Best Hikes
with
CHILDREN

MICHIGAN

MICHIGAN

JIM DUFRESNE

THE
MOUNTAINEERS
BOOKS

Published by
The Mountaineers Books
1001 SW Klickitat Way, Suite 201
Seattle, WA 98134

First edition, 2001

Published simultaneously in Great Britain by Cordee, 3a DeMontfort Street, Leicester, England, LE1 7HD

Manufactured in the United States of America

Project Editor: Christine Ummel Hosler
Editor: Jane Crosen
Maps: Jim DuFresne
Photographs: Jim DuFresne
Series Design: The Mountaineers Books
Layout: Mayumi Thompson

Cover photograph: *A waterfall in the Munising area*. Photo by Jim DuFresne
Frontispiece: *Pumping water at a state forest campground*. Photo by Jim DuFresne

Library of Congress Cataloging-in-Publication Data
DuFresne, Jim.
  Best hikes with children in Michigan / Jim DuFresne.— 1st ed.
    p. cm.
Includes index.
  ISBN 0-89886-493-3 (pbk.)
  1. Hiking—Michigan—Guidebooks. 2. Family recreation—Michigan—
Guidebooks. 3. Michigan—Guidebooks. I. Title.
  GV199.42.M5 D83 2001
  917.7404'44—dc21
                                                                2001001435
                                                                CIP

To Michael and Jessica,
Because the small footprints in the dunes
blow away so quickly.

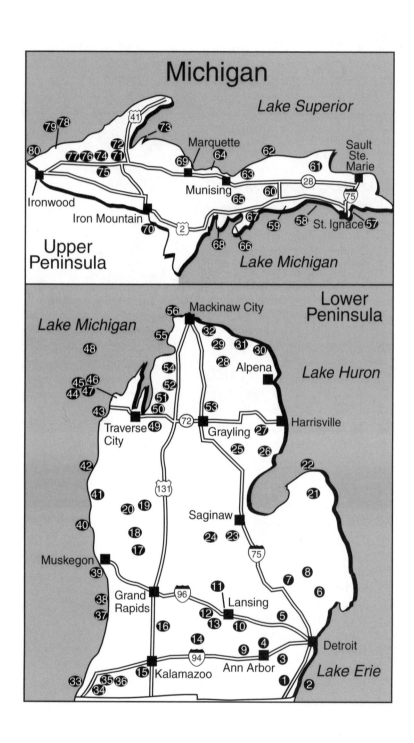

CONTENTS

Legend

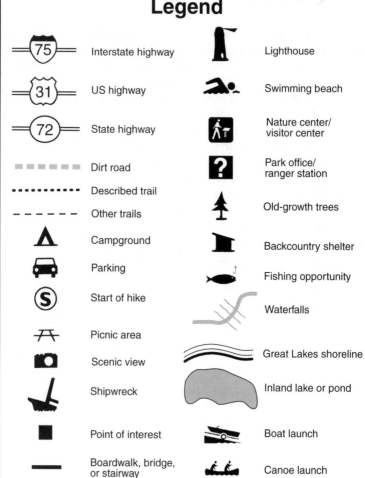

75	Interstate highway
31	US highway
72	State highway
Dirt road	
Described trail	
Other trails	
Campground	
Parking	
S Start of hike	
Picnic area	
Scenic view	
Shipwreck	
Point of interest	
Boardwalk, bridge, or stairway	

Lighthouse	
Swimming beach	
Nature center/ visitor center	
Park office/ ranger station	
Old-growth trees	
Backcountry shelter	
Fishing opportunity	
Waterfalls	
Great Lakes shoreline	
Inland lake or pond	
Boat launch	
Canoe launch	

FOREWORD

Whatever the season or wherever travelers might find themselves in Michigan, a hiking adventure is just around the corner.

That's especially true when experiencing the outdoors with youngsters. They don't need much—a modest trail, a final destination, a pack with a few treats, and a spirit of fun supplied with a smile from Mom and Dad.

Jim DuFresne has been traipsing around Michigan's natural highlights with his youngsters for some time now, writing about his experiences for *The Saginaw News* and seven other Booth newspapers in the state. His collection of some of his favorite hikes deserves a place on bookshelves—or better yet, in backpacks—of all parents who like to share outdoor experiences with their children.

In addition to his knowledge about the outdoors, Jim's love for having fun with his children is obvious. If you have the book, you've taken the first step. The next one takes a little more effort.

Get out and enjoy some Michigan hiking adventures with your children. Years from now, your youngsters will cherish the special times you had together.

Ken Tabacsko, Feature Editor
The Saginaw News

ACKNOWLEDGMENTS

After three years of venturing into the woods, it finally happened at the end of Jessica's sixth summer. While I was tying her younger brother's shoes on a trail in Sleeping Bear Dunes National Lakeshore, Jessica announced she was going to start back to camp . . . on her own. She quickly climbed over a low, wooded dune, hiked 50 yards down the trail, and then suddenly realized that nothing surrounded her but trees . . . no signs, no buildings, no other people, no Daddy.

It was probably the first time she had ever been in the woods all by herself, and it was a little scary. So Jessica sat down in the middle of the trail and sang to herself until we came walking over the dune.

"I decided I'd better wait to make sure you guys were all right."

I suppressed my smile, told her everything was fine, and then asked her if she could lead us back to camp. My daughter immediately took her position at the front and marched off, the proudest trail leader I've ever seen.

Kids—they're as natural in the outdoors as they are in a Saturday matinee. After many grand wilderness adventures around the world—scaling peaks, walking glaciers, and running wild water—I've concentrated the past few years on showing my children a slice of Michigan along short trails and on overnight backpacking trips. Reaching a 12,000-foot pass in New Zealand is fine, but I've never regretted a moment spent observing a deer with my daughter or seeing the excitement burst from my son after he's lifted his Mickey Mouse fishing rod and discovered a small bluegill on his hook.

If children have slowed me down, it was only to observe things I have missed too often in my hurry to reach the peak.

I deeply appreciate all the assistance from my editors at The Mountaineers Books, who encouraged me to write this book, as well as the editors at Booth News Service—Meegan Hollan, Dennis Tanner, and Phil Moldenhauer—in Lansing, who launched my statewide column about taking children outdoors, called "Kidventures." I am also indebted to the Venture Outdoor editors of the Booth Newspapers, particularly Howard Meyerson of the *Grand Rapids Press* and David Graham of the *Flint Journal*, who faithfully have been running the column and encouraging me to keep seeking out wonderfully short hikes and adventures for children.

Most of all, these summers couldn't have been possible without the help of Jessica and Michael DuFresne and all the other children I have walked, hiked, and backpacked behind.

INTRODUCTION

Somebody gave me a nudge, and I lazily opened my eyes and lifted my head. It was my daughter, and she said, "Dad, the beach is ours again."

So it was. The pair of hikers who had appeared briefly at the other end were gone. Once again Jessica and I were the only occupants of this long stretch of sand that bordered the turquoise waters of Lake Michigan and looked toward sand dunes towering in the distance.

It was quite a place, and on this late August afternoon, it was all ours. We were on an island paradise, and from the beach it could have passed easily for a remote spot in the South Pacific. But we had never left Michigan. I discovered South Manitou Island when I went searching for little adventures. My then five-year-old daughter had been car camping but never backpacking. This was her first experience at hiking into a campground with some gear on her back, and I

wanted to make sure it was a good one. Her pack had to be light, which meant mine was going to be heavy. Small price to pay for a happy camper. The hike had to be short, no more than 2 miles to our destination.

But most of all, it had to be adventurous enough to keep her mind off weary legs. South Manitou Island fit the bill nicely, and eventually I discovered many special places in Michigan that do. Looking to expose your children to the outdoors? Michigan is a great state to do it. The opportunities for short hikes, fun walks, and easy backpacking adventures are almost unlimited.

The eighty outings compiled in this book were chosen because they represent a variety of trails and a wide range of physical challenges for children, from easy

Hiking to Lake Michigan along the Platte Plains Trail.

strolls to climbs to commanding views. But most of all, these trips cover the best scenery Michigan, a state blessed with a treasure of natural jewels, has to offer. That's the key. It's not enough just to choose a short, level trail for a youngster's first hike. It's better to choose a longer one if it includes viewing a shipwreck, walking along a lakeshore, or watching frogs leap into a marsh. Keep the mind active, and the legs never tire as quickly.

These hikes are geared for children ages three to ten. It's been my experience that most children are ready to begin easy 1- or 2-mile hikes after they are three. By the time they reach adolescence, ages ten to thirteen, children can work up to hikes of 9 to 10 miles, with the proper pretrip conditioning and mild days at the beginning of each expedition. Many will be able to carry not only their personal gear in a backpack but a share of the group equipment. At this point, for all practical purposes, children can join their parents on almost any outing in Michigan. That makes the three-to-ten-year age period crucial in developing an appreciation, even a never-ending love, for the outdoors and hiking.

Setting an agreeable pace on the trail is important, but most unsuccessful family outings result from poor planning, not fast walking. You need to study the proposed outing carefully, the mileage involved each day, the type of terrain that will be covered, and other factors, such as "Will it be buggy?" Then look at the younger members of your party and decide whether they can handle the hike comfortably.

MICHIGAN'S GEOGRAPHY, GEOLOGY, AND WEATHER

Thanks to the Great Lakes, Michigan is composed of two peninsulas that are shaped like a hand holding a mitten. Four of the five Great Lakes—Lake Superior, Lake Michigan, Lake Huron, and Lake Erie—surround the state and have turned its border into 3200 miles of lakeshore. Michigan is not only outlined by blue, but it is also inundated with water. Stand anywhere in the state, and you are no more than 6 miles from one of its 11,000 inland lakes or 3600 miles of streams and rivers.

The Lower Peninsula—the mitten—is 285 miles from north to south and 195 miles from east to west. This half of the state features a topography of low rolling hills in the south, a 1200- to 1500-foot plateau in the north, and wonderful sand dunes along the Lake Michigan shoreline. These mountains of sand often rise 200 to 300 feet above Lake Michigan and are the most extensive collection of

Hiking on the Lake Michigan shoreline along the Platte Plains Trail

freshwater dunes in the world. This is Michigan's "dune country," and it makes for intriguing topography and outstanding hiking.

Lake Michigan also features the best swimming in the state. Known as the "Golden Coast," the beaches are wide and sandy, the water warms by mid-July, and there are numerous public parks where you can spend a day at the beach. You can swim in any of the Great Lakes, but keep in mind that most of Lake Huron in Michigan features a rocky, gravel shoreline, while Lake Superior is usually too cold, even in the middle of the summer, for swimming or wading.

Among the best places to swim in Lake Michigan or to hike in the dunes are P.J. Hoffmaster State Park (see Hike 39), Silver Lake State Park (Hike 40), Nordhouse Dunes Wilderness (Hike 42), and Sleeping Bear Dunes National Lakeshore, one of three national park units in Michigan (Hikes 43 through 48).

Michigan's other two national parks—Isle Royale and Pictured Rocks—are located in the Upper Peninsula, the hand connected to the mitten by the 5-mile-long Mackinac Bridge. The Upper Peninsula is a heavily forested and lightly populated area that stretches 325 miles from east to west and is bordered to the north by Lake Superior.

This is Michigan's most isolated and in many ways its most spectacular region. Near Munising are the famed Pictured Rocks, multicolored sandstone bluffs and formations that rise more than 200 feet above Lake Superior (Hike 63). The most rugged corner of the state is Porcupine Mountains Wilderness State Park, a 60,000-acre tract of steep ridges and escarpments (Hikes 78 and 79).

The Upper Peninsula's trademark, however, is waterfalls, more than 200 of them. The largest one, the third largest cascade east of the Mississippi River, is Upper Tahquamenon Falls (Hike 61) north of Newberry, which measures more than 200 feet across. Other thundering cascades include Piers Gorge (Hike 70) near Iron Mountain, Sturgeon Falls (Hike 74) southwest of Baraga, and Black River Falls (Hike 80) north of Bessemer.

Passing through the middle of Michigan is the 45th Parallel, the halfway point between the Equator and the North Pole. This accounts for the state's pleasant climate and its four distinct seasons. Spring in the Lower Peninsula arrives by mid- to late April, and, depending on the year, there is often good hiking in April and May. Streams may be swollen and the trails muddy in places, but the wildflowers are blooming in profusion while ducks and geese are migrating through the region. Temperatures at this time of year can be cool, 50 to 60 degrees, and the bugs don't start appearing in mass until late May.

Summer, June through August, is the traditional hiking season in Michigan when kids are out of school, campgrounds are bustling, and temperatures can range from 70 degrees in the Upper Peninsula to the upper 90s in southern Michigan. The best time to hike is the fall, September to early November. Almost three-quarters of the state is hardwood forest, resulting in spectacular autumn colors that rival those in New England. Temperatures are cool, averaging 60 degrees, campgrounds are empty, and the trails are yours for the afternoon.

The hiking season ends on November 15, the first day of the state's firearm deer season. It's best to avoid state forests, national forests, recreation areas, and other public lands that allow hunting during this popular 16-day season. By December snow has fallen in many parts of the state, and hikers and families trade their hiking boots for skis, snowshoes, and sleds.

HOW TO USE THIS BOOK

Each hike begins with a trip synopsis—a block of information that shows at a glance the location, the type of hike and difficulty, the trail distance, any fees, and where to call for more information. Most of the time, a quick look at the synopsis will tell you if this is the outing you are looking for.

The most common hikes are "day hikes," walks that range from 1 to 5 miles to natural attractions such as lakes, waterfalls, viewpoints, or sand dunes. "Overnights" are hikes that offer opportunities for backcountry camping. "Interpretive walks" feature either display plaques or an accompanying brochure that examines the natural history of an area.

By far the most important category is "difficulty," in which each walk is rated "easy," "moderate," or "challenging." Because children grow at different rates and develop coordination and motor skills at different times, they can be anywhere in a wide range of ages before they are ready to undertake a "moderate" or "challenging" level of physical endurance. To successfully introduce children to the outdoors, it's crucial to know their limits and abilities. I've seen some five-year-olds tackle 6 rugged miles on Isle Royale National Park and others who are drained after a walk around the block.

Easy: Most of these hikes and backpacking trips range from 1 to 2 miles a day. The terrain is predominantly level, provides easy footing, and can be handled by most children ages three to five. At this age children have a short attention span, so hikes with a variety of scenery have been selected. Many are interpretive walks, with numbered posts that correspond to information in brochures, an excellent choice for a child's first hike. Plan on frequent stops and more than an hour to cover a level mile of trail with a three-year-old.

Moderate: Physical endurance, motor skills, and attention span have improved greatly for children ages six to eight, and most should be able to handle a moderate-rated outing. Hikes and backpacking adventures in this category range from 3 to 5 miles, but parents still need to plan numerous snack and water breaks for short rests, as well as a long lunch break. Children can also handle steeper climbs, especially some of the sand dune country on the west side of the state.

Challenging: Children who are nine to ten years old are capable, with proper conditioning, of covering 6- to 8-mile hikes or steep grades to high points like those found in Porcupine Mountains Wilderness State Park. They are also quite agreeable to spending numerous days in a tent away from home, making a week-long adventure to Isle Royale National Park possible. Regardless of age, all children are intrigued by wildlife and the natural world around them, but at this stage they are old enough to visualize the course on a map, keep track of miles, and pace themselves mentally to reach a goal like a trailside camp at the end of a day.

Each trip synopsis is followed by a description of the trail itself—not every foot of the path, but steep climbs to consider, panoramas not to be missed, and points of interest to ponder for a minute or two. The text also describes spots along the route where you can turn around or loop back to shorten the trip, as well as places that make for scenic rest stops or snack breaks. With children, this is important information to have, as the inevitable question during the hike will be "How much farther until we stop for lunch?"

Most of these descriptions also include a map; in many instances, this is the only one you might need. If more detailed maps are desired, you can use U.S. Geological Survey 7.5-minute series topographic quads (scale: 1 inch equals 2000 feet). The best place to purchase topos of Michigan is from the Michigan United Conservation Clubs by contacting MUCC Map Center, P.O. Box 30235, Lansing, MI 48909; phone 800-777-6720. You can request a "Map Source Index," which lists all the topos that cover the state.

TAKING CHILDREN OUTDOORS
Day Hiking
A simple walk in the woods is often the best start to a lifetime of adventure outdoors. Read about a hike and then use the information to motivate children at the beginning. Tell them you're going to see a waterfall, a lighthouse, trout rising to the surface of a clear stream, or freighters plying the waters of the Great Lakes. A little excitement at the start goes a long way toward motivating young hikers. After that wears off, or after you've passed the shipwreck, be prepared to bribe them with "energy food" (candy and sweet snacks to some people). It's the old carrot-on-the-stick trick. Tell them that in 15 or 20 minutes you'll stop for a snack, and then dole out just enough so there's some left over for the next break.

Children learn quickly that being "the leader" is an important and even prestigious role. The younger hikers should always lead, forc-

Picking wild berries

ing older members of the party to adjust to their pace. Rotate this leadership role, however, or you might have a major dispute on your hands. Emphasize to the leader and every child in the group the importance of not running, a tendency that is always strong among children, especially those under the age of five. That run-and-stop, run-and-stop pace will wear them out quickly. Tell kids, or even force them if need be, to walk in a slower but steadier stride. Soon they will learn that this is the best way to hike a trail.

Although high-tech hiking boots are available even for toddlers, the vast majority of the trails described here do not require such expensive footwear. Sturdy tennis shoes and thick socks are sufficient for the "easy" and "moderate" hikes in this book, and when a hike needs more than that, it's spelled out clearly in the text. During the summer, bring plenty of energy food, sunscreen, insect repellent, even long-sleeved shirts and pants if it's the height of the bug season (late June to early August). Most important, don't forget the water bottle. Children, especially those under the age of five, are much more vulnerable to heat stress than adults and should drink water often on the trail.

Schedule not only rest stops, snack breaks, and a lunch period, but also time for frequent stops along the trail—to observe ducks in a pond, a spider's web glistening with the morning dew, or a golden mushroom popping through a layer of wet leaves. This is when children learn to appreciate the outdoors and respect their environment. I'm often amazed at the end of an adventure to learn that my son's high point of the day wasn't the view from the top of the ridge, but an inchworm he saw crawling on a leaf.

Pass along your outdoor experience and observations, praise young hikers for how long they've walked or how high they've climbed, and be patient. Give children the time to inspect and examine this new world around them.

Backpacking

Even a three- or four-year-old can go backpacking, if his or her parents are willing to carry the gear in. Place a small daypack on the child's back, stick a coat or another piece of clothing inside that will give the pack some bulk but not much weight, and there will be few problems with an overnight hike into the woods. If a young hiker can undertake a 1- or 2-mile day hike, then a 1-mile walk into a backcountry campground, many of which are described in this book, should be no problem. The important aspect of backpacking is the lesson that you can survive with everything strapped to your back. It doesn't take children long to learn the simplicity of survival. Plus, when they return the next day to see the car (security) still there, they swell with a tremendous sense of accomplishment.

Children in the range of six to eight years of age can begin carrying much of their own gear, as long as their packs don't exceed twenty-five percent of their body weight. They should also be carrying their own water and learning how to ration it over the course of the day. From ages nine to ten, children should be able to carry all their own gear, plus a small portion of group equipment. They should now be able to handle some simple camp tasks on their own, such as gathering firewood, filling up the water bottles, or inserting the stakes in a free-standing tent.

In many ways children are like adults when it comes to backpacking. They need to have raingear, hats, insect repellent, extra clothing, and warm jerseys or sweaters. They get as cold in wet jeans as anybody else, and at dinner time, after hiking 4 miles in the woods, kids are going to be as hungry as you are. The biggest mistake I make with my children is underestimating how much their appetites increase while backpacking. We're forever fighting over the last ravioli in the pan.

Camping

Many of the trails in this book begin at or near a campground, making a weekend of camping and hiking a popular activity in Michigan. The Michigan state park system offers more than 14,000 sites, most of which feature electric hook-ups, showers, heated restrooms, and other such conveniences. Such facilities make a weekend away from home considerably easier for the kids, as well as for Mom and Dad. A modern campground teaches children the first lesson of camping: It's possible to have fun without television, video recorder, boom box, or toys within arm's reach.

But I prefer taking my children to the rustic campgrounds found in many state parks and scattered throughout the state forests, national forests, and national parks and lakeshores in Michigan. These are less crowded, with spacious sites in a much more wooded setting. The most difficult part about such rustic facilities isn't getting children to sleep on the floor of a tent. After a day of fresh air and vigorous activity, most, unlike their parents, nod right off, even without the aid of sleeping pad. The most difficult part might be getting them to use the vault toilets. Be patient with them when it comes to "toilets with no handle."

Setting up camp in the Horseshoe Bay Wilderness

For the child who is apprehensive about spending a night in a tent or in the woods, a good way to ease into camping is to try one of the mini-cabins that can be rented in state parks or the tipis available through the Rent-A-Tipi program. The tipis, especially, seem to capture the imagination of children, who spend a weekend fantasizing about the Old West as opposed to worrying about being away from their bedrooms. A dozen parks feature the authentic-looking, 24-foot-high tipis, which inside have cots and, just outside, a picnic table and a fire ring. Call the Michigan State Department of Natural Resources, Parks and Recreation Division, for a list of parks that offer the program (phone 517-373-9900). Mini-cabins, Rent-A-Tipis, and campsites in Michigan state parks can be reserved in advance through the central reservation system at 800-447-2757 or online through the Michigan Department of Natural Resources website at *www.michigandnr.com*.

When camping, bringing some toys is necessary, especially bedtime Teddy. But don't overload the car by hauling in the toy box. For most young campers, finding a feather on the ground or a grasshopper on a plant will inevitably make up for whatever toy was left at home.

Fishing

The trails and campgrounds mentioned in this book provide ample opportunities for children to try their hand at fishing before, after, or sometimes even during the hike. Children under the age of sixteen do not need a Michigan fishing license; all others do.

Kids are naturally drawn to fishing, even if they don't have the attention span the sport requires. For that reason it is best to start from the shore or a dock and equip them with a short rod and closed-face reel or even a cane pole. Rig the line with a good-sized bobber, some weight, and a hook with whatever bait happens to be available—worms, crickets, or grasshoppers. This setup will work well with panfish, the easiest fish for a young angler to pursue.

The key is to teach them to keep an eye on the bobber and to "set the hook," with a hard upward swing of the rod, when the bobber begins to dip—not such an easy lesson for a three- or four-year-old to learn. But many of the fishing opportunities mentioned in this book are lakes with good stocks of panfish. A calm evening in mid- to late summer will bring schools of bluegill, sunfish, and pumpkinseed near the shore, and a well-placed bobber will soon be dipping enough to maintain the interest of most children. Catching a big northern pike or walleye is fine, but as far as kids are concerned, hooking a bucketful of panfish is better, even if they are too small to keep.

THE TEN ESSENTIALS

For activities such as hiking and backpacking—when you and your family are away from the car or the campground—The Mountaineers has developed a list of the "Ten Essentials," equipment that should be carried on every major outdoor outing.

1. **Extra clothing.** Weather can change quickly, and for a child to be caught in a rainstorm without a change of clothing or a jacket could be a serious situation.
2. **Extra food.** A hungry child is one who plods along, making an unexpectedly lengthy hike last even longer.
3. **Sunglasses.** The sun can be blinding on snow, water, and especially on a windblown sand dune.
4. **Knife.** No one should go anywhere without a good pocket knife.
5. **Firestarter.** Either a chemical fuel or even the stub of a candle can be used to start a fire and provide warmth if you have to delay your return.
6. **Waterproof matches.** The firestarter isn't much good without a way to light it.
7. **First-aid kit.** It doesn't have to be the entire wing of a hospital, but your kit should include enough supplies to cover most mishaps.
8. **Flashlight.** For those outings when you don't quite make it back to the car before sunset.
9. **Map.** On longer hikes and overnight backpacks, such as South Manitou Island, a guidebook can never replace a good map.
10. **Compass.** A map is of little use unless you have a compass and the ability to orient yourself.

SAFETY

We all want to enter the woods and come out safely. Hiking, canoeing, skiing, and all other forms of backcountry travel entail a certain amount of risk, especially when children are involved. No guidebook, no matter how well researched and written, can alert you to every hazard or anticipate your abilities and limitations. In the end, you alone are responsible for your own safety and that of those in your party.

But risks can be minimized and most mishaps avoided if you are prepared before you head out, and alert once you are on the trail. Be conscious of your drinking water. The best bet is to carry a water bottle and not depend on any untested source to quench a thirst. Regardless of whether it is from Lake Superior or a small trout stream, all water in Michigan should be considered affected by *Giardia lamblia* (an intestinal parasite). If you do need to use water from a lake or river, either boil it for one full minute or run it through one of several filters on the market today, which are designed to remove the parasite.

In addition to staying well hydrated to avoid heat stress, you should also be aware of the hazards of hypothermia and its symptoms, even during summer trips. Because of their small body size, children are more vulnerable to exposure and a drop in the body's internal temperature than are adults. A child with the first stages of

Great Lakes Visitor Center in Ludington State Park

hypothermia is often listless, unwilling to cooperate, and whiny. Then the common physical signs, such as uncontrolled shivering, set in. Be alert to any of these signs and work quickly to rewarm the young hiker with food, hot drink, additional clothing, or an extended break in a sleeping bag.

Less threatening are sore feet and bug bites, but they can ruin a trip just as easily. It is best to solve potential foot problems before the hike by selecting the proper boots or tennis shoes and then making sure they fit and are broken in. But always carry a supply of moleskin and bandages for when a blister suddenly develops 2 miles from the trailhead.

Also pack insect repellents, as well as long-sleeved shirts, pants, and hats during the summer to combat mosquitoes, no-see-ums, deerflies, and blackflies. Most important, on overnight trips have a tent with insect screening that has been double-checked for even the tiniest hole. You can survive bugs during the day as long as you have a safe haven to escape from them at night.

TEACHING OUTDOOR ETHICS

Children emulate their parents. If you have a genuine love for the outdoors, it doesn't take long for them to begin enjoying day hikes, camping trips, or a backpacking adventure into any of Michigan's many wild areas. If you show a fear of bears, snakes, or other wildlife, your children will soon come to detest those animals as well. All this should be kept in mind when you're heading outdoors, for what you teach and display in the first few years will set a pattern for the rest of your children's lives.

I loathe trash on the trail or a beer bottle in the river, and it wasn't long before my daughter said the only thing worse than a biting deerfly was a litterbug. By age five she was pouncing on trash left lying in the middle of a campsite and teaching her younger brother to do the same.

Show them how to leave a backcountry campsite as though it had never been there to begin with. Teach them not to litter, disfigure campground facilities, or bathe in a lake. Explain to them that the most beautiful trees are the ones without names, hearts, or arrows carved in the bark. Tell them that everything you pack in, you pack out, because there are no "trash days" in the wilderness.

Help them to see the beauty of wildlife and thus develop a respect for the other animals that share the woods. Lead them to a quiet stand of hardwoods, a world without man-made noise, and then sit back while they hear their first leaf fall. Spend a moment on a trout stream, where the water is so clear and unpolluted, you can watch mayflies hatch on the surface or fish dart below.

Such simple discoveries now will make for permanent judgments later. Who knows? A child's walk in the woods while holding Dad's hand may be just enough to save a forest in the future.

A NOTE ABOUT SAFETY

Safety is an important concern in all outdoor activities. No guidebook can alert you to every hazard or anticipate the limitations of every reader. Therefore, the descriptions of roads, trails, routes, and natural features in this book are not representations that a particular place or excursion will be safe for your party. When you follow any of the routes described in this book, you assume responsibility for your own safety. Under normal conditions, such excursions require the usual attention to traffic, road and trail conditions, weather, terrain, the capabilities of your party, and other factors. Because many of the lands in this book are subject to development and/or change of ownership, conditions may have changed since this book was written that make your use of some of these routes unwise. Always check for current conditions, obey posted private property signs, and avoid confrontations with property owners or managers. Keeping informed on current conditions and exercising common sense are the keys to a safe, enjoyable outing.

The Mountaineers Books

KEY TO SYMBOLS

 Day hikes. These hikes can easily be completed in a day or part of a day. Camping along the trail is not recommended or is prohibited.

 Backpack trips. Overnight camping is permitted along the trail in designated areas (some with structures or facilities), or a public campground is within reasonable walking distance of the hiking trail. In every case, the campground or camping area appears on the accompanying map.

 Easy trails. These are relatively short, smooth, gentle trails suitable for small children or first-time hikers.

 Moderate trails. Most of these are 2 to 4 miles total distance and feature more than 500 feet of elevation gain. The trail may be rough and uneven. Hikers should wear lug-soled boots and be sure to carry the Ten Essentials (see Introduction).

 Difficult trails. These are often rough, with considerable elevation gain or distance to travel. They are suitable for older or experienced children. Lug-soled boots and the Ten Essentials are standard equipment.

 Hikable. The best times of year to hike each trail are indicated by the following symbols: flower—spring; sun—summer; leaf—fall; snowflake—winter.

 Driving directions. These paragraphs tell you how to get to the trailheads.

 Turnarounds. These are places, mostly along moderate trails, where families can cut their hike short yet still have a satisfying outing. Turnarounds usually offer picnic opportunities, views, or special natural attractions.

 Cautions. These mark potential hazards—cliffs, stream or highway crossings, and the like—where close supervision of children is strongly recommended.

 Viewpoint. These are places with exceptional views.

Opposite: *Family closely examining Paint Creek along the Paint Creek Trail*

SOUTHEAST MICHIGAN

1

LONG BARK TRAIL

Location ▪ Oakwoods Metropark
County ▪ Wayne
Type ▪ Interpretive walk
Difficulty ▪ Easy
Hikable ▪ March to December
Length ▪ 2 miles
Fee ▪ Vehicle entry fee
Information ▪ Oakwoods Metropark Nature Center,
734-782-3956 or 1-800-477-2757

Oakwoods Metropark is a 1700-acre unit of the Huron-Clinton Metropolitan Authority, which oversees a system of thirteen parks along the watersheds of the Huron and Clinton Rivers. Oakwoods includes a stretch of the Huron River just upstream from the Flat Rock Dam. Here the Huron is a sluggish waterway filled with marshy islands and small bayous, a perfect place for waterfowl and bird life to gather.

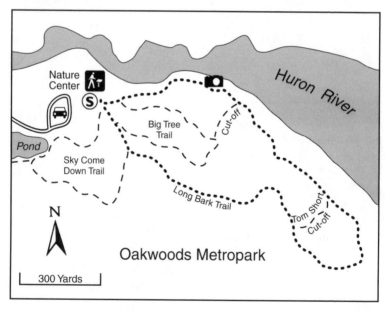

Viewing the Huron River from the Long Bark Trail

Most of the river lies in a 400-acre Nature Study Area accessed by almost 4 miles of trails and featuring a nature center. All four loops are interpretive trails, but Long Bark is the longest at 2 miles and the most interesting walk, as a portion of it follows the Huron River. The theme of the trail is forest ecology, and its fifteen numbered posts correspond to an interpretive brochure available at the nature center.

The park is located in the southeast corner of Wayne County and is reached from I-275 by departing at exit 13 and heading east on Sibley Road. Turn south (right) on Huron River Drive and follow it 4 miles to Willow Drive. The park entrance is just west on Willow Drive. It's a 2-mile drive along the park road to the parking lot and nature center.

A visit to the Oakwoods Nature Center is a good introduction to the trail. There are several excellent hands-on displays inside as well as exhibits of live animals. One of the exhibits is a huge turtle pond where more than a dozen turtles will be lazily swimming through the water or climbing onto a large rock to sun themselves under a heat lamp. An interpretive panel informs you that they include painted turtles, blandings turtles, and red-eared slider turtles, and that the big one, the mean-looking one sitting on the bottom, is a snapper. The center is open from 10:00 A.M. to 5:00 P.M. daily in the summer. During the school year the hours change to 1:00 to 5:00 P.M. on weekdays and 10:00 A.M. to 5:00 P.M. weekends.

Pick up Long Bark Trail just outside the nature center. The loop is hiked in a clockwise direction, and you begin in the woods but quickly arrive at a bluff overlooking the Huron River. What lies below you is a maze of oxbows, marshy islets, and winding channels where you can view a variety of bird life through binoculars: blue herons, egrets, kingfishers, even osprey.

The trail follows the edge of the bluff, passing a couple of benches overlooking the river and then a spur to Big Tree Trail within 0.3 mile from the nature center. At this point the trail swings into the mature hardwood forest of beech, maple, and oak.

You pass Tom Short Cut-off 0.75 mile from the nature center, and shortly after that the trail begins looping back. Now the trail is completely out of view of the river, plunging deeper into the forest for most of the second half. You pass junctions to both Sky Come Down Trail, a 1-mile loop, and Big Tree Trail, a 0.75-mile walk, just before returning to the nature center.

2 CHERRY ISLAND MARSH TRAIL

Location ■	Lake Erie Metropark
County ■	Wayne
Type ■	Day hike
Difficulty ■	Easy
Hikable ■	March to January
Length ■	1.5 miles
Fee ■	Vehicle entry fee
Information ■	Lake Erie Metropark office, 734-379-5020 or 800-477-2757

Lake Erie Metropark is a 1607-acre unit of the Huron-Clinton Metropolitan Authority and a state-designated Wildlife Viewing Area. The metropark preserves a tract of marshland at the mouth of the Detroit River, making it a strategically important resting place for birds crossing Lake Erie.

Visitors can spot a variety of bird life including great blue herons, egrets, bald eagles, and ospreys. The park is renowned among birders for its fall migration of hawks. In most years birders will sight more than 100,000 broad-winged hawks during migration.

The park's newest path, built in 2000 at a cost of more than $550,000,

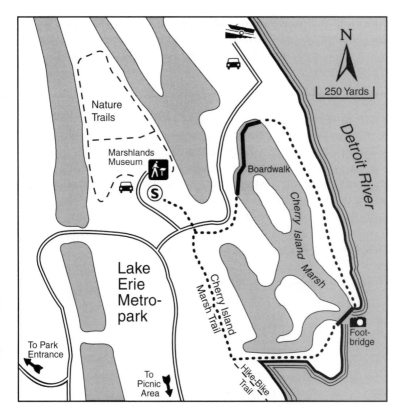

is Cherry Island Marsh Trail—a 1.5-mile loop around Cherry Island, a mat of cattails in the middle of a marshy lagoon. Almost a third of the trail is a boardwalk that skirts the wetlands. There is hardly any place along this loop where you can't stop and scope out the marsh in search of birds or other wildlife, particularly in spring and fall.

Lake Erie Metropark is east of Rockwood. To reach the metropark from I-75, depart at exit 29 and head east on Gibraltar Road for 2 miles. Turn right (south) on West Jefferson Avenue, and you'll reach the park entrance within 2 miles.

Begin the hike with a visit to the park's Marshlands Museum and Nature Center. Inside you can study mounts of the birds you might later spot or learn about the heritage and history of duck hunting in this region of Michigan they call "Downriver." The interpretive center is open during the summer from 10:00 A.M. to 5:00 P.M. daily. During the school year the hours are 1:00 to 5:00 P.M. on weekdays and 10:00 A.M. to 5:00 P.M. weekends.

Outside the museum, pick up the park's paved bike path, which forms the first leg of the loop. Within 0.3 mile you leave the asphalt and, heading east, follow a dike along the edge of the lagoon to an impressive bridge. The footbridge arches high across a channel where the lagoon empties into the mouth of the Detroit River. In the middle of the bridge there is an observation area, and for good reason: The view from the middle of the bridge is spectacular. To the south you see the Detroit River flowing into the watery horizon of Lake Erie. Looking north you see Cherry Island and the marsh, alive with waterfowl.

From the bridge the trail heads north along a narrow strip of land that allows you to tightrope between the crashing waves of the Detroit River and the protected lagoon. The trail skirts the edge of the park's boat launch area and then, turning west, becomes a boardwalk. For more than 0.25 mile, the boardwalk follows the northern end of Cherry Island Marsh and serves as an excellent vantage point for birdwatching. Eventually the trail reappears and crosses the park road to return to the nature center.

3 NORTH BAY TRAIL

Location ▪ North Bay Park
County ▪ Washtenaw
Type ▪ Day hike
Difficulty ▪ Easy
Hikable ▪ March to January
Length ▪ 1.5 miles
Fee ▪ Vehicle entry fee
Information ▪ Township of Ypsilanti, 734-484-0073

At North Bay Park, a small Ypsilanti Township park, you can "walk" across the water, stopping anywhere along the way to enjoy the view or to fish. The water is Ford Lake, a 975-acre impoundment of the Huron River just southeast of Ann Arbor.

The park is only 15 acres, squeezed in between I-94 and Ford Lake, yet contains almost 2 miles of trail. That's because half of the loop winds across the north end of the reservoir, via boardwalks and bridges between small islands, making it both an interesting place to hike and a haven for shore anglers.

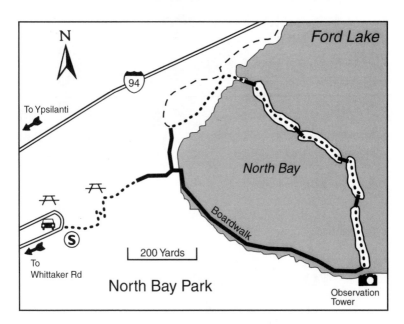

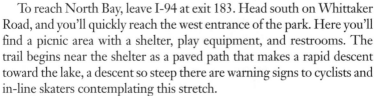

To reach North Bay, leave I-94 at exit 183. Head south on Whittaker Road, and you'll quickly reach the west entrance of the park. Here you'll find a picnic area with a shelter, play equipment, and restrooms. The trail begins near the shelter as a paved path that makes a rapid descent toward the lake, a descent so steep there are warning signs to cyclists and in-line skaters contemplating this stretch.

Within 0.25 mile you enter a marsh and continue east on a boardwalk that leads you out onto Ford Lake. For a park so small, this is an impressive boardwalk. It edges the shoreline for almost 0.5 mile, allowing boatless anglers to either cast among the lily pads along the shoreline or toss their bait into the deeper water on the other side. Most budding anglers catch bluegills, black crappies, and occasionally a largemouth bass.

The wooden path ends at a two-tier observation tower from which you can take in a sweeping view of this 3-mile-long lake. Beyond the tower you begin island-hopping north and west across the middle of North Bay via four man-made islands connected by bridges. Each island has picnic tables and large shady trees where you can plop down, cast out your lines, and enjoy a cool breeze off the lake.

A mile from the trailhead you step off the fourth island and return to the mainland. At the junction, head left (west). Within 0.25 mile

Young angler fishing from a dock

you return to the boardwalk and follow the paved path back to the west entrance.

4 DOLPH PARK NATURE AREA

Location ▪ Ann Arbor
County ▪ Washtenaw
Type ▪ Interpretive walk
Difficulty ▪ Easy
Hikable ▪ March to January
Length ▪ 0.5 mile, round trip
Fee ▪ None
Information ▪ Ann Arbor Department of Parks and
Recreation, 313-994-2780

A day in the university town of Ann Arbor can be a busy one for a family, with visits to the Ann Arbor Hands-On Museum, the U of M's Exhibit Museum to look at dinosaurs, or Matthaei Botanical Gardens. But one stop should always be Dolph Park Nature Area.

The small park began as a 26-acre gift from Ralph Dolph to the city in 1962 and over the years has been enlarged to a 44-acre preserve that protects the only two natural lakes in the area. Dolph is a rather amazing spot. Within the city limits of Ann Arbor is a natural hideaway complete with bridges, overlooks, and trails that wind around lakes, ponds, streams, and marshes.

There is also wildlife, and that's why Dolph is an excellent stop for children. Thanks to the wide range of habitats, children will be charmed by what bounces across the trail in front of them or what they might spot among the cattails. Even if they don't see the animals themselves, they can often spot the tracks, particularly in spring and after a fresh snowfall. Dolph is a great place to introduce children to tracking.

To reach the park, leave I-94 at exit 172 on the west side of Ann Arbor and head west on Jackson Road. Within a mile turn south on Wagner Road, and you'll see the park entrance posted on the left. Dolph Park Nature Area is open from 6:00 A.M. to 10:00 P.M. daily.

Begin your outing by spending a few minutes at Dolph's outdoor interpretive area, just off the small parking lot, where display panels explain the importance of the wetlands, describe the upland communities, and show how glaciers formed both First Sister and Second Sister Lakes. A panel on tracks not only shows you the prints you might encounter—ringneck pheasants, red squirrels, cottontail

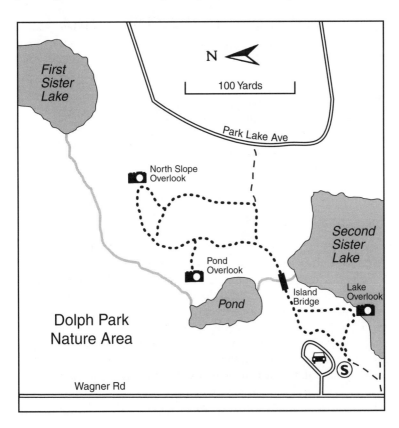

rabbits, raccoons, weasels—but also tells you what you can learn about the animal from its walking pattern.

To follow the trail system in a counterclockwise direction, head due east from the interpretive area to the Lake Overlook on the edge of Second Sister Lake. Both lakes are kettleholes, the result of large blocks of ice breaking off the glacier and being buried by sand and debris. When the ice finally melted, the lakes were formed. Second Sister Lake is the younger of the two and not aging (filling in with sediment) nearly as fast as First Sister Lake.

The side loop quickly rejoins the main trail and arrives at Island Bridge, which crosses an outlet stream of Second Sister Lake. The main trail then climbs out of the woods and swings north in an old field to arrive at North Slope Overlook, 0.25 mile from the interpretive area. The overlook is on a low bluff where you have a good view of First Sister Lake and the dead forested wetland that is slowly filling it in. A little farther down the trail is Pond Overlook. At either overlook you can sit quietly and be rewarded with a glimpse of waterfowl or other wildlife, especially if you arrive at dusk. From the pond, the trail loops back to Island Bridge and returns to the parking area.

5 WILDWING TRAIL

Location ■	Kensington Metropark
Counties ■	Oakland and Livingston
Type ■	Day hike
Difficulty ■	Easy
Hikable ■	March to January
Length ■	2.5 miles
Fee ■	Vehicle entry fee
Information ■	Kensington Metropark headquarters, 248-685-1561 or 1-800-477-3178

Kensington Metropark can be a zoo at times—for the wrong reasons. On a holiday weekend, it's overflowing with joggers, boaters, and family get-togethers. But even then you can find areas within the 4337-acre park to escape the crowds and heat, stroll along a shaded forest trail, and view a variety of wildlife. In the northwest corner of the park is Kensington's nature study area, featuring an interpretive

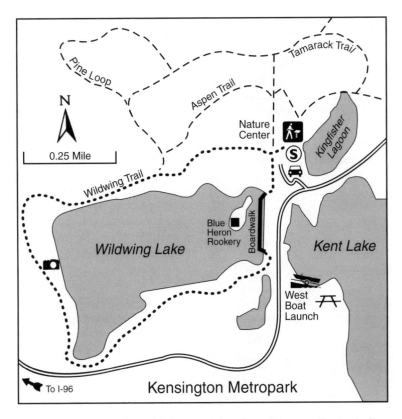

Pine Loop

Tamarack Trail

Aspen Trail

N

0.25 Mile

Nature Center

Kingfisher Lagoon

Wildwing Trail

Blue Heron Rookery

Boardwalk

Wildwing Lake

Kent Lake

West Boat Launch

To I-96   Kensington Metropark

center, several ponds and lakes, and 8 miles of foot trails, including one that skirts the edge of Wildwing Lake.

Wildwing Trail is an easy 2.5-mile hike that can be accomplished in tennis shoes. Along it you'll spot a variety of wildlife, from chipmunks to mute swans and other waterfowl, to any of the numerous white-tailed deer living in the park. Wildwing is marked by more than a dozen interpretive plaques explaining such subjects as dying lakes, glaciers, and the importance of wetlands. When combined with a visit to the nature center, the hike makes for an educational experience as well as a short outdoor adventure for children. If this path is too long, there are six shorter trails that range from 0.5 mile to 1.8 miles.

The park straddles the Oakland–Livingston county border and can be reached from I-96 by departing at Kensington Road (exit 151) or Kent Lake Road (exit 153), just east of US-23. Head north on either, and signs will direct you to the park entrance and the nature center.

Swans in Wildwing Lake, Kensington Metropark

The nature study area has its own parking area, and on the way to the interpretive building you pass Kingfisher Lagoon and its carp pond on the west end. The huge fish can be seen lazily swimming during the summer, and a plaque explains their arrival in the United States. The nature center contains an exhibit room with an active beehive, freshwater aquariums, exhibits of other cold-blooded animals, and several hands-on displays. The building is open from 10:00 A.M. to 5:00 P.M. Tuesday through Sunday and from 1:00 to 5:00 P.M. on Monday.

All trails depart from the center, and along Wildwing Trail you quickly come to a junction with Aspen Trail and the rock viewing area, where an interpretive display shows and explains the differences between metamorphic, sedimentary, and igneous rocks. The trail skirts the marshy shore of Wildwing Lake, then moves into an impressive maple-oak forest, and in 0.5 mile reaches the second access point to Aspen Trail. Located here is a small pavilion with benches overlooking the lake and a hand pump for water.

Beyond the rest area, Wildwing Trail crosses a meadow and then becomes a narrow forest trail that climbs to a footbridge in 0.6 mile. You remain on the low bluff and reach the halfway point of the hike, a large observation deck overlooking the lake. Benches and the view make this an ideal spot for a short break.

Wildwing Trail descends sharply from the overlook and swings around the southwest corner of the lake, breaking out near the park road across from the golf course at one point. But that is only a brief intrusion, and the path quickly swings away from the cars and pavement to stay close to the shoreline. Almost every step along this section offers a view of the lake, and in midsummer the hundreds of greater white lily flowers are dazzling. So are the resident mute swans—huge birds, with adults often weighing 20 pounds or more. You'll also pass what at first appears to be somebody's treehouse built above the lake. Interpretive signs will inform you that the large wooden structure is actually a hacking box, used to reintroduce osprey to the area.

A second footbridge is reached 2 miles from the beginning, at which point the trail becomes a wide boardwalk that extends 0.2 mile along the east side of the lake. Built in 2000 at a cost of $250,000, the boardwalk puts you out on the lake and allows for easy wildlife viewing. Peer into the shallow waters to look for bluegills and painted turtles, or bring a pair of binoculars to view the swans, mallards, and other waterfowl on the surface. At the north end of the boardwalk you pass a small island that during the spring is a blue heron rookery with usually more than thirty nests. From the boardwalk you merge onto a service drive back at the rock display area.

6   PAINT CREEK TRAIL

Location ■	Dinosaur Hill Nature Preserve
County ■	Oakland
Type ■	Day hike
Difficulty ■	Moderate
Hikable ■	March to January
Length ■	2.4 miles, one way
Fee ■	None
Information ■	Dinosaur Hill Nature Preserve, 248-656-0999; Paint Creek Cider Mill, 248-651-8361

It's hard to believe that in the middle of Oakland County, one of the fastest-growing areas of Michigan, there is a 9-mile wooded path winding along a trout stream. Paint Creek Trail, which runs from Rochester to Lake Orion, was the first rail-trail project to be completed in the state. Leftover railroad artifacts from the Penn Central Line—including rails, wood ties, even communication boxes—still litter the area, but now the raised bed is an avenue of escape from the boom and construction of northern Detroit.

The entire trail makes for a long day, too long for most children, but one stretch lies between a nature center in Rochester and a cider mill to the north, ideal places to begin and end an afternoon outing. This 2.4-mile hike is along the trail's most scenic section, where it frequently crosses Paint Creek, a stream stocked annually with trout. The wide, level path is most spectacular during the fall colors of October, when you can view the autumn reds and oranges of hardwoods and then end the walk with a jug of freshly squeezed apple cider. The mill is also the place to drop off a car if you don't want to backtrack to Rochester.

Dinosaur Hill Nature Preserve, named after a hill that children said looked like a sleeping dinosaur, is located on the northern edge of Rochester and is bordered on one side by Paint Creek. The 16-acre preserve is reached from Rochester Road (Main Street in town) by turning west

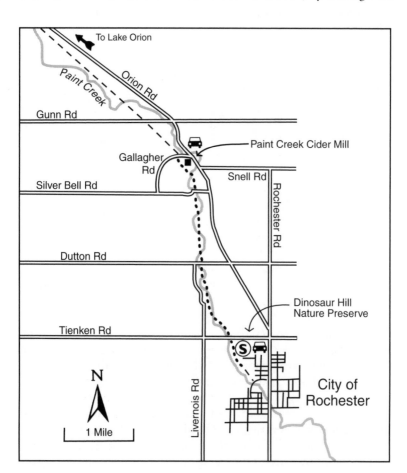

onto Woodward for two blocks and then north on Oak Street to North Hill Circle, where the entrance is posted to the west. Dinosaur Hill includes an interpretive center, three self-guided nature trails, and quick access to Paint Creek. Hours are 9:00 A.M. to noon Monday, 9:00 A.M. to 5:00 P.M. Tuesday through Friday, and 10:00 A.M. to noon on Saturday.

One of the nature paths leads to Paint Creek Trail, which heads north on the west bank of the river. You immediately come to Tienken Road and on the north side cross a bridge over the creek. There are houses within view of the trail at first, but gradually you leave the sights and sounds of Rochester behind to wander through the woods with the trout stream gurgling beside you. This is greater metropolitan Detroit? Amazing. Within a mile of the nature center you cross the creek a second time and pass a series of steps leading down to the water—good place for a break.

Two more bridges are crossed, one on each side of Dutton Road. A few more bridges and 2 miles from the nature center, the trail approaches Silver Bell Road. Just before the road, the banks of the creek have been reinforced with logs, the work of a local Trout Unlimited chapter. Logs and rocks have been used to stabilize eroding portions of the stream, which were making the water too silty for trout eggs to hatch. Natural reproduction now occurs and, combined with annual plantings, makes Paint Creek a popular destination for anglers who bait small hooks with worms and occasionally pull out rainbow trout up to 15 inches in length.

On the north side of Silver Bell Road, the trail becomes a wide gravel path that parallels the creek. The stream swings close to the path several times, and 2.2 miles from the start you come to another set of steps that overlook an S-bend in the creek. It's a scenic spot to sit and whittle the afternoon away, especially if you brought a pole and a can of worms along. If it's July, tell the troops to keep an eye out for wild raspberries, which grow along this stretch of the trail. A ripe berry is a real find, however. Between the abundance of birds in the area and passing hikers, few berries hang on the bush for very long.

Just before reaching Gallagher Road, you see the backside of Paint Creek Cider Mill along the stream. The historic mill, located on the corner of Gallagher and Orion Road in the community of Goodison, is best known as a fine restaurant. But from September through Christmas the mill makes apple cider and sells it from a stand outside that is open from 9:00 A.M. to 6:00 P.M. Friday and Saturday and 9:00 A.M. to 5:00 P.M. on Sunday. During the summer they sell ice cream from the stand, and for children either is a welcome treat after conquering Paint Creek Trail.

7 LAKESHORE AND SPRINGLAKE TRAILS

Location ▪	Independence Oaks County Park
County ▪	Oakland
Type ▪	Day hike
Difficulty ▪	Moderate to challenging
Hikable ▪	March to December
Length ▪	2.4 to 3 miles
Fee ▪	Vehicle entry fee
Information ▪	Independence Oaks County Park office, 248-625-0877; Lewis E. Wint Nature Center, 248-625-6473

Independence Oaks County Park is the largest unit in the Oakland County Parks system at 1062 acres, and a state-designated Wildlife Viewing Area. The park encompasses rolling hills, wooded ravines, the headwaters of the Clinton River, and a variety of wildlife including white-tailed deer. But the centerpiece is Crooked Lake, a 68-acre lake with crystal-clear water that is free from the buzz of motorboats and jet skis.

The park has a 10-mile network of trails, mostly in a rugged, undeveloped area on the west side of the lake. Here Springlake Trail and a portion of Lakeshore Trail can be combined to make a 3-mile loop that begins near the Lewis E. Wint Nature Center and leads you across the park's highest ridges and along Crooked Lake.

Keep in mind the hike does include more than 100 feet of climbing along an old glacial moraine that forms the main ridge in the park. If that is too much for your family of hikers, skip Springlake Trail and just walk Lakeshore Trail, an easy 2.4-mile loop that hugs the entire shoreline of Crooked Lake.

Independence Oaks is located near the village of Clarkston and can be reached from I-75 by departing at exit 89 and heading north on Sashabaw Road for 4 miles. Once inside the park, follow signs to the nature center.

Enlarged to 8300 square feet in 1997, Lewis E. Wint Nature Center is now one of the most impressive facilities in southeast Michigan. The new exhibit area leads you through four theme rooms devoted to water, the sun, weather, and geology. Water is by far the most intrigu-

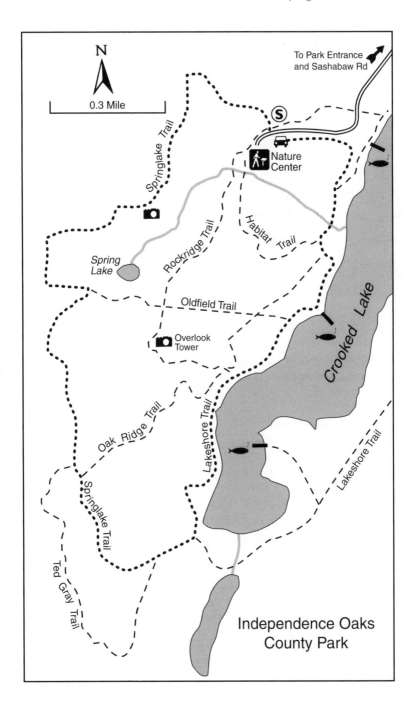

N

0.3 Mile

To Park Entrance
and Sashabaw Rd

Springlake Trail

Ⓢ

Nature
Center

Rockridge Trail

Habitat Trail

Spring
Lake

Oldfield Trail

Crooked Lake

Overlook
Tower

Oak Ridge Trail

Lakeshore Trail

Lakeshore Trail

Springlake Trail

Ted Gray Trail

Independence Oaks
County Park

Sunset along the Lakeshore Trail in Independence Oaks County Park

ing room, where a darkened atmosphere and rising bubbles make children feel as if they're underwater in a pond. The walls are aquariums filled with the wildlife they would see if they took a swim in Crooked Lake: bass, bluegill, frogs, and a very large and active snapping turtle.

The nature center is open daily 10:00 A.M. to 6:00 P.M. from Memorial Day to Labor Day, and Tuesday through Sunday 10:00 A.M. to 5:00 P.M. the rest of the year.

A trailhead with a map box in the nature center parking area marks the junction of Springlake and Rockridge Trails. Springlake leaves north (straight) and begins with a descent to a long boardwalk across a marsh. From this sea of cattails the trail climbs the ridge known as North Hill, descends briefly, then climbs again, topping out at a bench 0.5 mile from the parking lot. If the leaves aren't too thick, you can view the entire marsh area, which stretches from Spring Lake to Crooked Lake.

The trail quickly resumes climbing and then follows the ridgeline, rising and dropping with its crest, until reaching the posted junction with Oldfield Trail a mile from the nature center. Head down Oldfield Trail a few steps for a view of Spring Lake through a stand of tamarack. The small pond is a dying lake, slowly being filled in and covered up by the carpet of moss and bog plants that encircles it.

At the junction Springlake Trail curves sharply away from the lake and begins a steady climb to the crest of another ridge known as South Hill. You follow the ridgeline for a short spell before topping out at a posted junction with Ted Gray Trail. You are now standing at almost 1200 feet, more than 150 feet above the lake. At this point Springlake Trail curves to the southeast and begins a descent from South Hill that quickly becomes a sharp drop. You bottom out at the junction with the return of the Ted Gray Trail and then, 2 miles from the nature center, reach Lakeshore Trail and a view of Crooked Lake. Head left (north) at the junction.

Lakeshore Trail skirts the south end of the lake, a small, shallow bay that attracts both waterfowl and anglers in the spring. The lake supports bass and northern pike but is best known for its panfish. At one point the trail climbs to a picnic table on a small knoll overlooking the lake, a great place for a snack.

About 2.5 miles into the hike, you reach a floating fishing pier. From the dock children can often watch mallards or Canada geese using the lake surface like a runway. If it's late April or May, have them search the clear water for the sandy craters of spawning bluegill or other panfish. Find one of these underwater "dishes," and usually the protective mother is nearby.

If it's mid- to late summer, pack a rod and reel and try fishing for panfish here or at one of the many docks on the west side of the lake. Use a simple bobber rig with a leaf worm or half of a nightcrawler, which can be purchased from the park boathouse. Young anglers rarely will catch a "keeper" off the docks, but the action is lively.

From the fishing dock, Lakeshore Trail continues north and stays within view of the lake; Habitat Trail merges into Lakeshore Trail from the left. Shortly you'll cross a bridge over the creek from Spring Lake, and Habitat Trail will split off from Lakeshore Trail. Follow Habitat Trail to the left, and in a few hundred yards you'll be back at the nature center parking lot.

8   GRAHAM LAKES

Location ■	Bald Mountain Recreation Area
County ■	Oakland
Type ■	Day hike
Difficulty ■	Moderate
Hikable ■	March to December
Length ■	3.6 miles
Fee ■	Vehicle entry fee
Information ■	Bald Mountain Recreation Area headquarters, 248-693-6767

Northern Oakland County can be a surprisingly rugged area, and the best example of this is Bald Mountain Recreation Area. There is no actual "Bald Mountain" in the state recreation area, but the trail

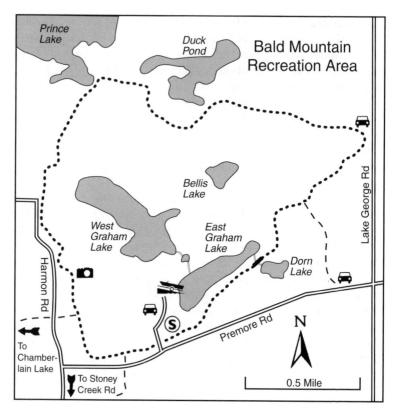

system in the park's northern unit does climb and descend a number of ridges and hills, and to young hikers these are mountains indeed. The 8-mile network is composed of three main loops and is popular with mountain bikers and cross-country skiers who like the challenge of the hilly terrain.

But the Graham Lakes Loop, a 3.6-mile walk, is also one of the better day hikes for children in the metropolitan Detroit area. The adventure includes good ridgetop views, along with almost a dozen lakes and ponds in the lowlands, where such wildlife as grouse, cottontail rabbits, Canada geese, and possibly even a deer can be spotted. Come spring the patches of wildflowers around the wetlands are extensive, and in the autumn the ponds are highlighted by fall colors of hardwood trees. Summer is nice, too, but remember that these stagnant bodies of water are natural hatcheries for mosquitoes, especially late May through June.

The northern unit of the recreation area is located east of Lake

Orion and can be reached from M-24 by following Clarkston Road, an especially scenic route where it forms an S-turn to cross Paint Creek. After 2 miles turn north on Adams Road, which ends at Stoney Creek Road. Head east 100 yards and then north on Harmon Road, which leads into the park. There are four trailheads and parking areas for the Graham Lakes Loop, including one at the end of Harmon Road.

A nice way to hike this trail is to begin at the East Graham Lake boat launch, which you reach by turning onto Premore Road from Harmon Road and heading east for 0.25 mile. By starting here and walking counterclockwise, you put the heavily forested stretch in the middle of the hike and save the best view for the end.

A large wooden display sign marks the trail, and hikers should head east from there. Within 0.5 mile you follow the south shore of East Graham Lake and then cross a wooden bridge over the stream that connects East Graham to Dorn Lake. The trail winds away from the lakes and enters the forest. Now, this is a hike. Within the next mile you climb up and over several hills, pass a handful of ponds, and pass within 50 yards of a trailhead on Lake George Road. You rarely break out of the trees until you reach one arm of Duck Pond.

The best view of the large pond is in another 0.5 mile, or 1.9 miles from the boat launch, where you ascend to a bench with Duck Pond to the north and the surrounding hills to the west. The trail emerges from the trees again when you come to Prince Lake, roughly the

Taking a lakeside break in Bald Mountain Recreation Area

halfway point and a logical spot for a snack and a rest. Avoid the trails that wander around the lake, and soon you'll enter a pine plantation whose towering trees are in perfect rows. In the middle is another bench.

Within 0.6 mile from Prince Lake the trail leaves the trees to pass a private home and then arrive at the posted trailhead at the end of the Harmon Road. The trail heads south from here, crosses a wooden bridge over a stream, and then begins to ascend. "Is this Bald Mountain?" somebody is bound to ask. Well, no, but to young hikers it does seem like climbing a peak. On the way up you pass a view of Shoe Lake to the west, and then you actually do "top out" at a clearing with a bench and a panorama of West Graham Lake and many of the surrounding ridges you've already walked over.

After a quick descent into open fields, you pass the posted junction to Chamberlain Lake, 0.5 mile from the Harmon Road trailhead. Swing east into the woods to emerge at the boat launch parking area within a few minutes.

Opposite: *Hiking in the Meridian Riverfront Natural Area*

HEARTLAND

9

BOG TRAIL

Location ■	Waterloo Recreation Area
County ■	Jackson
Type ■	Day hike
Difficulty ■	Easy
Hikable ■	March to January
Length ■	1.5 miles, round trip
Fee ■	Vehicle entry fee
Information ■	Gerald E. Eddy Discovery Center, 734-475-3170

Geology just wasn't cutting it with kids at the Waterloo Recreation Area. So the Gerald E. Eddy Geology Center was enlarged and its exhibits revamped and expanded. Then the name was changed. In 2001 the state park interpretive center, one of seven in Michigan, was unveiled as the Gerald E. Eddy Discovery Center.

What hasn't changed is the network of five short trails, all 2 miles or shorter in length, that depart from the center and wind through a variety of habitats. The longest is Oakwoods Trail, a 2-mile loop through an upland forest of oak and hickory that offers good views of Mill Lake. But the most unique trail is the Bog Trail, a round-trip walk of 1.5 miles to the floating bog that surrounds Cedar Lake.

The Discovery Center combined with a hike along the Bog Trail makes for an interesting afternoon for children, but keep in mind that bugs rule a bog in the summer.

The center is located in the east end of Waterloo Recreation Area between Jackson and Ann Arbor. Leave I-94 at exit 157 and head north on Pierce Road. Follow Pierce Road for 3.5 miles, then turn left (west) on Bush Road for 1.2 miles to the center's posted entrance.

Among the improvements at the Discovery Center are a new atrium to watch birds and other wildlife, a new classroom where naturalists hold weekly programs, and a new reception area and gift shop. But what children find most interesting are the new displays in the exhibit areas. In one room the high-tech, interactive displays include a glacier and ice cave video simulation, a "Mad Scientist's Mineral Lab," a computerized geology game, and a Make-A-Fossil table.

Hey! Isn't this geology? Sure, we're just not telling kids that.

In the second exhibit room the displays focus on natural history

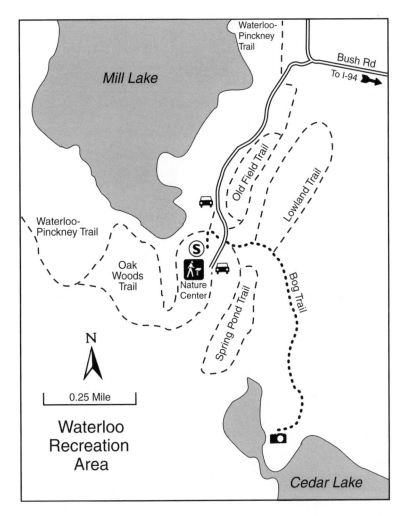

and the park's unique ecosystems. Take some time to examine the displays devoted to bogs, and then hit the trail.

From the Discovery Center, follow the footpath toward Bush Road. At the first posted junction the Bog Trail heads right and leads you across the entrance drive and back into the woods.

Within 0.25 mile you cross a bridge over a sluggish stream and then climb a small hill forested in some impressive beech and oak. On both sides of the hill are low-lying wet areas—bug factories, if you will—that the trail descends to and crosses on a boardwalk. In another 0.25 mile you pass a sign warning hikers that "Bogs can be dangerous!" and then reach a floating trail.

On the Floating Bog Trail at Waterloo Recreation Area

The reason for the warning is that under the grassy mat is deep mud and water. Stepping on the mat and breaking through would not only be messy but potentially hazardous. That's because the muck holds onto its victims, slowly pulling them down the more they struggle. Such was the fate of several mastodons, elephant-size animals that once roamed southern Michigan and were later uncovered by farmers in the area.

The floating trail, a wooden walkway, begins in a stand of tamarack but quickly breaks out to the open bog, a mat of unusual plants actually floating on an old lake. You can reach down and push on the bog as if it were a water bed. Bring a plant book or study pictures in the Discovery Center before beginning the hike, and you'll be able to identify a variety of rare orchids or even insect-eating pitcher plants. The trail ends at a small observation deck in the middle of the bog.

10 EASTGATE CONNECTION

Location ▪	Meridian Riverfront Natural Area
County ▪	Ingham
Type ▪	Day hike
Difficulty ▪	Moderate
Hikable ▪	March to December
Length ▪	2.7 miles, round trip
Fee ▪	None
Information ▪	Meridian Township Parks Office, 517-349-1200, ext. 330; Harris Nature Center, 517-349-3866

Eastgate Connection is a short trail, only 0.3 mile long, but an important one, linking two parks for an excellent family hike to an interesting interpretive center.

Eastgate Park and Harris Nature Center, along with Legg Park, are known collectively as the Meridian Riverfront Natural Area and lie side-by-side in protecting 200 acres of the forested floodplains and bluffs along the Red Cedar River. The various trails in each park are interconnected, forming a 4.6-mile system that follows the south bank of the Red Cedar River much of the way but crosses only one road.

The round-trip walk from Eastgate Park to the Harris Nature Center is only 2.7 miles, a distance even children as young as five or six can easily handle. The nature center is a perfect place to take an extended break before heading back, and at the end there are the facilities for a well-deserved picnic.

To reach Eastgate Park from Okemos, head east on Grand River Avenue for 4.5 miles. Turn south on Meridian Road, and pass the park's posted entrance within 0.5 mile.

From the trailhead, located in the parking lot, you begin on Beech Tree Loop. The trail immediately enters the woods and crosses a

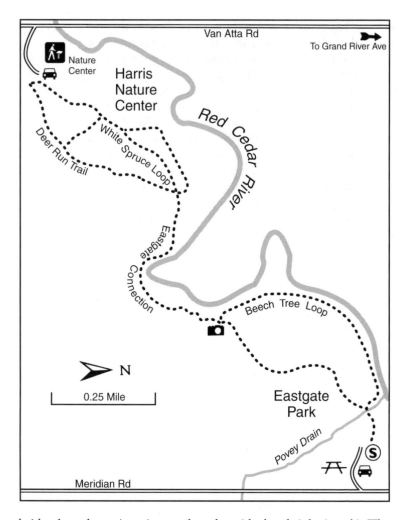

bridged creek to a junction on the other side; head right (north). The northern half of the loop traverses the lowlands along the Red Cedar River, weaving through a stand of grayish beech trees. In less than 0.5 mile you swing away from the river, climb a steep stairway, where there is an excellent view of the river, and arrive at the junction with Eastgate Connection. Head right (south).

This short connector path emerges from the woods and skirts the edge of a rather posh neighborhood. One home features a two-story garage, Greek columns around the pool, and a treehouse that is bigger than my first apartment. Strange scenery for a nature walk perhaps, but before you can think twice about it the trail enters the next park, and you are back in a more natural surrounding.

Within 0.3 mile Eastgate Connection arrives at a junction with both Deer Run Trail and White Spruce Loop. The 0.6-mile Deer Run Trail passes through old fields and pasturelands where in July a profusion of wild blackberries will be ripe for the picking. The 0.5-mile White Spruce Loop swings closer to the Red Cedar River but is never in view of the river. Both trails feature interpretive plaques and end at the nature center, 1.3 miles from the trailhead.

Harris Nature Center has bathrooms, a drinking fountain, and two display rooms. One room features the Preuss Water Exhibit, a scale model of the Red Cedar River, complete with running water, live fish, and a wraparound mural. There is also a wildlife observation room with a glass wall overlooking a bend in the Red Cedar River. The center is open 10:00 A.M. to 3:00 P.M. Tuesday through Friday, and 11:00 A.M. to 5:00 P.M. Saturday and Sunday.

For the return hike you can follow different trails through each park, backtracking only Eastgate Connection. You'll discover that the southeastern side of the Beech Tree Loop in Eastgate Park cuts through an upland bluff of hardwoods that encases the floodplains.

11 PLANET WALK

Location ■	Lansing River Trail
County ■	Ingham
Type ■	Interpretive walk
Difficulty ■	Easy to moderate
Hikable ■	Year-round
Length ■	1 to 4 miles, round trip
Fee ■	None
Information ■	Impression 5 Museum, 517-485-8115

Standing there, staring at the sun, we wondered how far we should go. Mars? Jupiter? My son's favorite planet, Uranus? "Hey, let's be daring and go where no man has gone before," I said in my best *Star Trek* voice. "Let's hike all the way out to Pluto." And off we went, walking from the heart of Lansing to the edge of the solar system along the cleverly simple but thoroughly enjoyable Planet Walk.

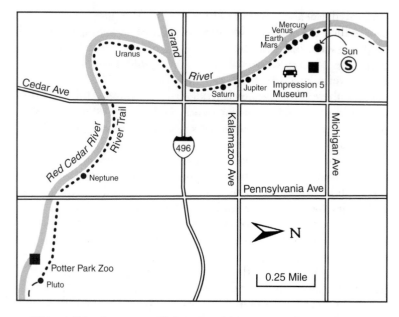

The trail is also very enlightening. Most maps of our solar system have condensed the distances in order to fit the sun and nine orbiting planets on the same page. You learn the names of the planets, you learn that Saturn has rings and that Jupiter has at least sixteen moons, but what you can't see or appreciate is the vastness of the system. Distances in the universe, the 93 million miles from the sun to Earth or the 3.7 billion miles to Pluto, are simply too large for children to comprehend.

That's why the Planet Walk was created. Sponsored and maintained by the Lansing Board of Water and Light, the walk is strung out along the Lansing River Trail, which follows the Grand and Red Cedar Rivers. You begin and end at two of Lansing's most enjoyable attractions, Impression 5 Museum and Potter Park. In between is a 45- to 60-minute walk from the sun to Pluto, a hike where every step represents a million scale miles.

To reach the start of the Planet Walk from I-496, exit at Pennsylvania Avenue and head north to Michigan Avenue. Turn left on Michigan and then left on Museum Drive just before you cross the Grand River. Impression 5 Museum is a block south on Museum Drive. One of the finest hands-on science centers in Michigan, featuring more than 200 exhibits on several floors, the museum makes for a natural place to begin or end any trek along the Planet Walk. Hours are 10:00 A.M. to 5:00 P.M. Monday through Saturday and noon to 5 P.M. on Sunday.

Located near the entrance of Impression 5 Museum is the sun, the start of the Planet Walk. Not only are the distances properly scaled along the walk, but so is the size and mass of each planet. That includes the sun, represented by a 20-inch golden sphere that looks like an overinflated basketball.

From there it's a few quick steps to the Mercury display. At this scale Mercury appears the size of a pencil eraser, while the plaque beneath it gives such vital information as its diameter, distance from the sun, and its mass compared to Earth. From the displays you learn that a year on Mercury is only 88 days long, that Mars has the largest known mountain in the solar system, and that Uranus might have once collided with another planet.

The first four planets are reached within a few hundred feet. But the rest are proportionally spread out, with nearly 0.75 mile between Saturn and Uranus alone. The largest planet, Jupiter, is 932 feet from the sun and the size of a small orange. The smallest, Pluto, the size of a pinhead on the trail, is located after the River Trail passes underneath Pennsylvania Avenue and enters Potter Park, home of Lansing's zoo. It's a one-way walk of 2 miles to Pluto, with the paved path hugging either the Grand River or the Red Cedar River most of the way.

Once at Pluto, the brochure notes that for you to reach the nearest visible star you would have to walk to the South Pole . . . a little too much for my son and me that day.

Studying the sun along the Planet Walk

12 DEER RUN AND TALLMAN TRAILS

Location ■ Lincoln Brick Park
County ■ Eaton
Type ■ Day hike
Difficulty ■ Easy
Hikable ■ March to December
Length ■ 2 miles
Fee ■ Vehicle entry fee
Information ■ Eaton County Parks, 517-627-7351

Lincoln Brick Park may contain only 90 acres and less than 3 miles of trails, but acre for acre it's as scenic and historically interesting as any park in central Michigan. The park's name comes from the Lincoln Brick Company, the last of five companies that made bricks here for more than a century until 1949. In the center of the park you can still view the remains of the brick factory's original boiler room, the warehouse where sand was stored, and a kiln that in its heyday was capable of producing 40,000 bricks a day.

The rest of the park is composed of heavily wooded bluffs that border more than 6000 feet of the Grand River and are crisscrossed by short footpaths. By combining Beechnut, Cherry Ridge, Deer Run, and Tallman Trails you can enjoy a scenic 2-mile loop.

The park is just west of Lansing. Leave I-96 at exit 86 and head south on M-100. Turn west on State Road for a mile and then drive south on Tallman Road to the entrance. Lincoln Brick Park is open daily from 8:00 A.M. to dusk.

Across the park road from the remains of the boiler room is the main trailhead and a map box. Head right (north) on Beechnut Trail. The path leads to a large footbridge over a ravine and then merges with Cherry Ridge Trail on the other side. Both trails put you on the edge of the bluff for an excellent overview of Michigan's longest river.

Both trails also wind past a series of knolls topped with trees and covered, in autumn, with fallen leaves. Closer inspection will reveal that the knolls are actually piles of discarded bricks with reddish chunks still poking out from between the leaves. When

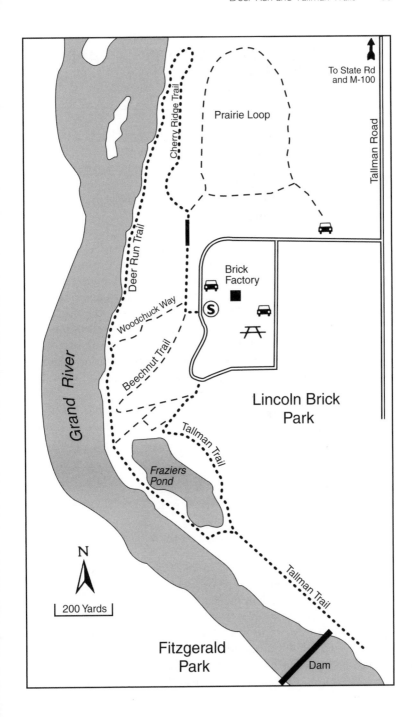

you make 40,000 bricks a day, you're bound to have a few bad ones. Other reminders from the park's brick-making days scattered along the trails include pieces of corrugated iron, a small brick-lined oven, even a mining cart that was used to carry shale up from the quarry.

In less than 0.5 mile from the trailhead, Cherry Ridge Trail descends to banks of the Grand River. Here you head left (south) along Deer Run Trail and within 0.5 mile reach Fraziers Pond. Legend has it that the brickmakers left a steam engine at the bottom of this quarry. Even if you can't see much in the murky water, the sandstone cliffs at the north end of the pond are almost as impressive as the famous Ledges in Grand Ledge (see Hike 13).

At 1.5 miles into the hike, Deer Run merges into Tallman Trail. To the left (north) Tallman Trail heads back to the park road, emerging near the old boiler room and other brick factory ruins. To the right (south) it skirts the Grand River for 0.25 mile, ending near the dam that spans the river between Lincoln Brick Park and Fitzgerald Park, Eaton County's largest unit.

In the fall you can watch fishermen wading this stretch of the river and casting for steelhead trout. There are also plans to eventually connect the two parks with a footbridge here that would allow hikers to continue to downtown Grand Ledge along the Ledges Trail (see Hike 13).

13 THE LEDGES

Location ■ Fitzgerald Park
County ■ Eaton
Type ■ Day hike
Difficulty ■ Easy
Hikable ■ March to January
Length ■ 2 miles, round trip
Fee ■ Vehicle entry fee
Information ■ Fitzgerald Park office, 517-627-7351

Grand Ledge, the only natural place to do any serious rock climbing in Michigan, also makes for a fun adventure for children, even if they're years away from lacing up a pair of rock shoes. The town west of Lansing is named after The Ledges, ancient sedimentary

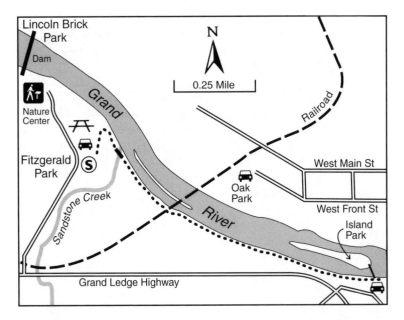

outcroppings that tower above the Grand River and have become a popular recreational and educational area.

Through much of the year, rock climbers gather at Oak Park on the north side of the river. But families should head to the south side for a far less dangerous adventure—a 2-mile, round-trip walk along the river that provides a close-up view of The Ledges.

One end of the trail is at Island Park, in the heart of downtown Grand Ledge. But the best place to start and end the hike is Fitzgerald Park, an Eaton County park located 1.5 miles west of town at 3808 Grand Ledge Highway. The 78-acre unit borders the Grand River and features six picnic sites, nature trails, a fish ladder, and a small nature center that is open May through October 1:00 to 5:00 P.M. on Wednesday, Saturday, and Sunday. On the other side of the park, just east of the barn theater, is the start of the Ledges Trail, marked by a box with interpretive brochures.

The first portion of the trail lies in the park and has eight numbered posts. You quickly descend a stairway and cross a bridge over Sandstone Creek to reach the first set of ledges on the other side. The impressive rock cliffs were formed 270 million years ago when most of Michigan was covered by water that carried and deposited sediments (sand, silt, and clay) in layers along river banks and beaches. After time and pressure compacted the layers into rock, the Grand River sculptured the cliffs through years of erosion.

Rock climbers scaling the Grand Ledges

Post number 8 is at the railroad trestle that marks the boundary of Fitzgerald Park. From here the trail crosses private property, and a couple of houses come into view above you. But most of the time the level trail is a secluded walk among hemlock pines with the Grand River lapping on one side and the stone cliffs on the other. At 0.5 mile, or the halfway point of the path, you can view the steepest ledges towering 70 feet above the north bank of the river. This is where most of the climbing activity takes place. With a pair of binoculars you can watch climbers slowly inch their way up the face, although the heavy foliage on both sides of the river blocks much of the view.

The trail ends at Island Park, where an old iron bridge crosses the river to the second island of what used to be the Seven Islands Resorts, a popular vacation spot at the turn of the century. Today the long, narrow island has benches, picnic tables, and small docks along the shoreline. There is also a waterfowl feeding area, where flocks of resident ducks eagerly await a handout.

If there are climbers on The Ledges, you can get a closer view of them by driving to Oak Park on the north side of the Grand River. The park is at the end of West Front Street off of M-100.

14 QUARRY BOARDWALK

Location ■	Keehne Environmental Area
County ■	Eaton
Type ■	Day hike
Difficulty ■	Easy
Hikable ■	March to January
Length ■	I mile
Fee ■	None
Information ■	Eaton County Parks, 517-627-7351

Located in the quiet little village of Bellevue is Dyer Kiln Historic Site, where you can see the remains of the first limestone kiln in Eaton County. In the 1800s the kiln was used to burn the rock for the production of cement, and among the buildings still held together by Bellevue mortar is Michigan's state capitol in Lansing.

The limestone used in the kiln was mined across the street in the West and East Quarries. The abandoned limestone quarries, long since flooded into small lakes, are today the centerpiece of Keehne

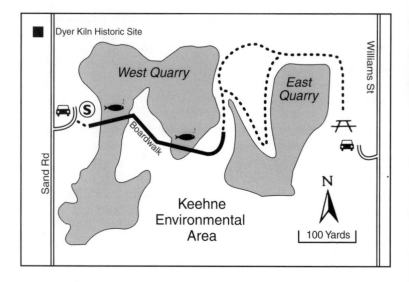

Environmental Area, an Eaton County park named for Edward Keehne.

At 17 acres, Keehne Environmental Area is not big, not developed with waterslides or playscapes, not even that well publicized. The park is simply a pleasant little place for a short hike where children can absorb the beauty of the woods, look for waterfowl and other bird life, or possibly catch a few fish.

From I-69, head west on M-78 into Bellevue. Once in town, turn left (south) on Sand Road where the Dyer Kiln is posted. The parking area for the west trailhead is just down the road from the historic site. Keehne Environmental Area is open from 8:00 A.M. to dusk.

From the trailhead on the west side of the park you immediately descend a long staircase. This is followed by a boardwalk almost a third of a mile long that first crosses the West Quarry and then skirts its southeast shore. If you are packing along fishing poles, this is the best place to use them. A variety of panfish and even northern pike can be caught in either lake, but the boardwalk doubles as a fishing pier where children can easily cast into the West Quarry.

From the east end of the boardwalk, a footpath continues past wildflowers and hardwood trees as it skirts the north end of East Quarry. You emerge at the east trailhead on Williams Street where there is a small picnic area with tables. From there you backtrack to Sand Road for a round-trip walk not much more than a mile in length.

WEST LAKE WETLAND WALK AND BOG WALK

Location ▪	West Lake Nature Preserve and Bishop's Bog Preserve
County ▪	Kalamazoo
Type ▪	Interpretive walk
Difficulty ▪	Easy to moderate
Hikable ▪	March to January
Length ▪	I to 3.5 miles
Fee ▪	None
Information ▪	Portage Department of Parks, 616-329-4522

West Lake Nature Preserve is only 110 acres. Walk more than 10 minutes, and you'll either be in a bog or a neighborhood. Located in the middle of the city of Portage, just minutes from I-94, the park is an upland hardwood forest bordered on three sides by either an extensive bog or West Lake.

Half of the park's trail system is the West Lake Wetland Walk, a mile-long interpretive loop with eighteen stops that was developed by the Kalamazoo Nature Center. The corresponding brochure, actually a small booklet, is one of the best interpretive guides I've come across and will help children have a better understanding of wetlands, "one of nature's most misunderstood resources."

If your family wants to cover more miles than the trails at West Lake offer, look for the trail that leads across South Westnedge Avenue, past the ball fields in South Westnedge Park to Bishop's Bog Preserve. Extending for a mile through this amazing 140-acre bog is a floating trail of plastic decking. The mile of interpretive trail combined with the round-trip walk through Bishop's Bog adds up to a 3.5-mile hike.

West Lake is a short drive from I-94. Depart at exit 76 and head south on Westnedge Avenue for 4 miles. Turn east on South Shore Drive; the entrance to West Lake is posted on the north side of the road.

From the West Lake trailhead near the picnic pavilion, an asphalt trail heads west and quickly arrives at a junction. Straight ahead is the trail to South Westnedge Park and Bishop's Bog Preserve. Turn right (north) to begin the West Lake Wetland Walk.

You begin in the woods but within minutes arrive at a floating

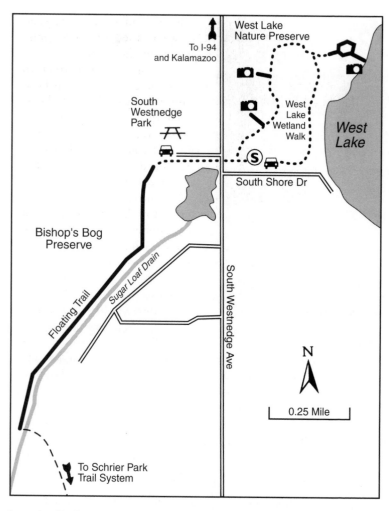

boardwalk that extends to an observation platform on an open bog. Here interpretive post number 3 explains how a "freshwater marsh is as productive as a tropical rain forest." At post number 5, the trail splits. Head left, and shortly you will arrive at a longer stretch of boardwalk to a second observation deck.

You return to the trail in the woods and shortly arrive at the most impressive portion of the walk: the third platform on the edge of West Lake. Departing east from post number 10 is almost 0.2 mile of bouncing boardwalk that leads you from the uplands hardwoods through a stand of tamarack and across the open bog that borders the lake's northwest corner. From the floating deck you can view this marshy corner

Hiking the floating trail in Bishop's Bog

of the lake and often in spring and fall see a variety of ducks gently bobbing on the water.

From the lake, backtrack to post number 10 and then head south. Shortly you'll reach the final interpretive post on the loop, number 18, and then trail signs will lead you the remaining 0.3 mile through the woods to the picnic pavilion.

To continue on to Bishop's Bog, follow the asphalt path west as it crosses South Westnedge Avenue, a busy street at times, and then skirts South Westnedge Park. Within 0.25 mile from West Lake you'll reach the north end of Bishop's Bog Trail. The trail to the bog soon becomes a floating path of plastic decking. Every 1000 feet there are benches where you can pause and take in the unusual scenery. The trail extends almost a mile through the bog. To return, simply backtrack to your vehicle at West Lake.

16 GRAVES HILL

Location ■	Yankee Springs Recreation Area
County ■	Barry
Type ■	Day hike
Difficulty ■	Easy to moderate
Hikable ■	March to November
Length ■	2 to 3 miles
Fee ■	Vehicle entry fee
Information ■	Yankee Springs Recreation Area headquarters, 616-795-9081

An old moraine makes a fine place for child's first "mountain climb" in southwest Michigan's Barry County. Graves Hill, the result of

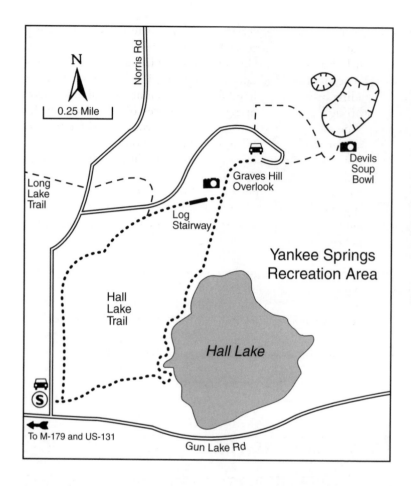

glacial activity, is located in the heart of Yankee Springs Recreation Area, one of the most popular units of the state park system. The loop trail is not strenuous but just steep enough to make children believe they're climbing a peak. The top rewards you with good views of the area, and the walk can be extended an extra mile to include Devils Soup Bowl, a deep depression.

Yankee Springs can be reached from Hastings by heading west on M-37, then turning onto Gun Lake Road for 10 miles. It can also be reached from US-131 by taking exit 61 and following county road A-42 east for 7 miles to its junction with Gun Lake Road. The park has several campgrounds, including a modern facility on Gun Lake. Because the 200-site campground is filled throughout much of the summer, it's considerably easier to obtain a site in the park's Deep Lake Campground, a rustic facility of 120 sites.

Hall Lake Trail is the loop to Graves Hill, and its trailhead is marked across from the entrance of Long Lake Outdoor Center. By heading up the right-hand fork of the immediate junction, you pass through pines and arrive at the shores of Hall Lake in 0.3 mile. Blue triangles mark the path, which crosses a bridge to skirt the lake for the next 0.25 mile, providing good views of the islands in the middle and any anglers who might be fishing for bass or bluegill.

At the northwest corner of the lake, the trail begins to climb gradually and then leaves the watery view for a sharper ascent to the high point. The steepest section is just before you reach the top, but even that can be handled by most five- and six-year-old children. It's a mile to the top of Graves Hill, marked by several large rocks, the largest of which is strategically placed so young hikers can obtain a better view. From the overlook you can see the wooded interior of the state recreation area and a portion of Gun Lake.

You can extend the hike another mile by descending to the parking

Angling for bass on Hall Lake at Yankee Springs Recreation Area

area nearby and following the park road. At the junction follow the right-hand fork along a wide, sandy trail. Within a half mile the trail ends at the edge of Devils Soup Bowl, a deep and very steep, wooded depression, also the result of glacial activity.

The return trail begins as a log staircase that descends sharply from the top of Graves Hill. Once you reach the bottom, a well-beaten path heads straight for the park road. But the trail swings left (southwest) into the woods. You hug the road briefly, even hike a ridge above it at one point, then swing away to pass a small meadow. Blue markers lead you through an impressive oak forest and past views of a larger meadow. Eventually the trail reenters pine forest and skirts the road the last 0.25 mile to the trailhead.

17 WETLAND TRAIL

Location ▪	NCCS Camp Newaygo
County ▪	Newaygo
Type ▪	Day hike
Difficulty ▪	Easy
Hikable ▪	April to November
Length ▪	2 miles, round trip
Fee ▪	None
Information ▪	Newaygo County Community Services, 231-924-0641

At the trailhead for the Wetland Trail at the NCCS Camp Newaygo is a sign that reads: "Walk At Your Own Risk!" My children loved it. Nothing like a day hike with a little adventure, even a degree of danger to it.

The Wetland Trail is a short but interesting walk through the heart of a bog and surrounding marsh. Access across the bog is along a boardwalk that was built in 1986 at a cost of more than $30,000. The boardwalk allows you to keep your feet dry but provides access into an area filled with life, including great blue herons, kingfishers, muskrats, raccoons, barred owls, and snapping turtles, along with pitcher plants and other insect-munching flora.

The risks? I'm not sure what they are, other than (if you arrived in June) mosquitoes so thick they form attack squadrons. This is a

Pausing along the Wetland Trail in Newaygo County

swamp hike best enjoyed in spring or fall and passed up during the summer.

The Wetland Trail is north of Newaygo. From M-37 turn west onto 40th Street, where the North Country Trail is posted. Within 2 miles turn south on Gordon Avenue and then east on 48th Avenue. A sign on 48th Avenue will direct you to the entrance and parking area of the Wetland Trail. Although located on NCCS camp property, the trail is open to the public daily April through November from dawn to dusk.

The boardwalk begins at the trailhead and quickly arrives at the first viewing platform. This one is at the edge of a bog, a small lake slowly being covered by a layer of sphagnum moss and other plants. Children are usually fascinated by what many refer to as the "quaking bog sensation," ground that bounces back up when they push on it.

Within 0.25 mile you reach a second viewing area, a group of benches located in a stand of dead trees. In the middle of this ghostly forest you can sit quietly, and within minutes the sounds of life will surround you: birds singing, crickets chirping, frogs croaking, a mallard landing in a patch of open water.

The trail continues from the second viewing area for a short spell until it reaches the marshy edge of Pickerel Lake. From the small lake you turn around and backtrack to the trailhead.

18 LODA LAKE WILDFLOWER SANCTUARY

Location ■	Manistee National Forest
County ■	Newaygo
Type ■	Interpretive walk
Difficulty ■	Easy
Hikable ■	March to December
Length ■	1.5-mile loop
Fee ■	Vehicle pass
Information ■	Baldwin Ranger District, 231-745-4631

My children and I stood near the edge of Loda Lake, looking for a splash of pink but finding only brown leaves. We were too early for color. But, though we had never been in the Loda Lake Wildflower Sanctuary before, we knew that in a few weeks a pink lady's slipper orchid would grace this spot. Post number 6 told us so.

A little way down the trail, post number 9 indicated sweetferns, and, my gosh, it was right. We dropped to our knees, and pushing up through last fall's decaying leaves were the small fiddleheads of this year's understory of ferns.

Originally part of a 1000-acre private reserve, Loda Lake was sold to the U.S. Forest Service during the Great Depression. Because of the wide variety of habitats found in a relatively small area, the USFS invited the Federated Garden Clubs of Michigan in 1938 to assist in creating a sanctuary for native plants, especially endangered and protected species, to ensure their survival.

Today the 72-acre preserve is still managed by the Federated Garden Clubs and over the years has evolved into a unique haven for botanists, wildflower enthusiasts, and families looking for a short but scenic hike. Winding through the sanctuary is a 1.5-mile loop with 39 numbered posts, keyed to an interpretive brochure, that mark the locations of plants. Most are wildflowers, and the trail guide informs you when they will be in bloom: early spring, sum-

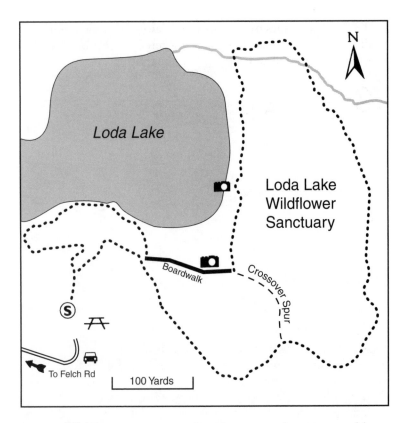

mer, or fall. If you stop to examine every one, plan on a good hour for the adventure.

To reach the sanctuary from White Cloud, head north on M-37 and then turn left on Five Mile Road where a sign for Loda Lake Wildflower Sanctuary is posted on the corner. Head a mile west and then turn right on Felch Road. The entrance to the sanctuary is a mile to the north. A daily, weekly, or annual Huron-Manistee Recreation vehicle pass is required to park at the Loda Lake trailhead. You can purchase one in White Cloud at Brohman One Stop at 7586 Woodbridge Road or in Baldwin at the Baldwin Ranger field office at 650 North Michigan Avenue.

The Loda Lake trailhead is located in a small picnic area that includes tables, a few grills, vault toilets, and a box with interpretive brochures. The trail guide is so important that at the end of the summer it's best to call ahead and have one mailed to you rather than trust your luck on the map box being stocked.

Fiddleheads pushing up through the ground

You soon encounter the first numbered post, near the junction with the return loop. Head left at the junction to continue following the posts in numerical order. The trail skirts the shoreline of Loda Lake and then uses a boardwalk to cross a wetland. Along the way you pass posts pointing out everything from pink lady's slipper and blueberries to wild lily-of-the-valley, bug-eating sundew, and swamp rose.

At the east end of the boardwalk there is a junction with a cross-over spur that shortens the walk to 0.5 mile. There is also a bench in the middle of the boardwalk and another one farther up the trail on the east end of Loda Lake. From the second bench the trail revisits the lake and then swings inland to begin its return. It's 0.75 mile back to the picnic area, and along the way you pass a fern marsh, two pine plantations, and an old orchard from when the area was being farmed in the 1930s.

19 PINE FOREST PATHWAY

Location ■ Pere Marquette State Forest
County ■ Lake
Type ■ Day hike
Difficulty ■ Easy
Hikable ■ April to November
Length ■ 1-mile loop
Fee ■ Camping fee
Information ■ Baldwin Office, Department of Natural Resources, 231-745-4651

Some people will hike miles to be able to sit on the banks of a trout stream free of docks, cabins, or any other man-made intrusions. Others will drive six or seven hours to peer up at the lofty crown of a 150-year-old pine. My son and I did both, and we were just a few hundred yards from our campsite. Better still, we were only a 10-minute drive from Jones's Ice Cream Parlor in Baldwin, our favorite place to get a double dip of Mackinac Island Fudge.

Both the trout and the trees are part of Pine Forest Pathway, which begins in Bray Creek State Forest Campground, part of the Pere Marquette State Forest. The rustic facility has ten sites overlooking the confluence where Bray Creek flows into the Baldwin

River. The campground is only minutes from "downtown" Baldwin, yet is secluded in a wooded setting of its own. Pitching a tent in the campground, hiking the trail, and indulging in Jones's homemade ice cream afterward are a northern Michigan ritual for my children and me.

Bray Creek is reached from US-10, 2 miles east of Baldwin. Turn north on Forman Road and then west on 40th Street. The campground is on 40th Street just after a bridge across the Baldwin River.

Pine Forest Pathway, posted in the back of the campground, begins as an old logging road among a stand of oak and jack pine that were planted in the 1950s. But within a few hundred yards you leave the two-track for a footpath that descends a wooded bank and becomes a delightful walk through a forest of red and white pine. Within 0.4 mile you reach the junction with the return loop; head left (south).

Shortly you'll be standing on the banks of the Baldwin River. This is the segment of the trail that is popular with anglers, as it parallels the trout stream for a short spell. The Baldwin River is your classic

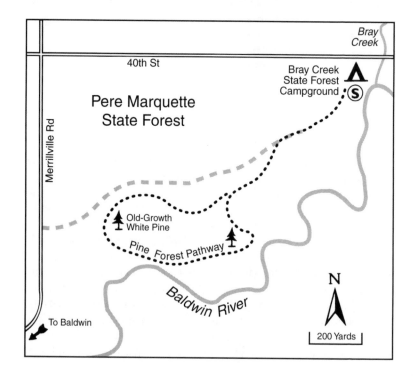

northwoods setting, a gently flowing stream 20 to 30 yards wide with a bank lined by cedars and bushy saplings.

Watching trout rise on the river is nice, but even more amazing to children will be the trail's namesake trees. The old-growth white pines are unexpectedly tall, and two of them feature interpretive signs. One, 35 inches in diameter, was snapped halfway up when struck by lightning. The other began growing before Michigan gained statehood in 1837, and today has a diameter of 31 inches and is more than 100 feet in height.

From the Baldwin River the trail begins to loop back toward the campground and within 0.25 mile arrives at the junction. You backtrack the first segment of the trail to return to the trailhead.

20 BOWMAN LAKE TRAIL

Location ■	Manistee National Forest
County ■	Lake
Type ■	Day hike or overnight
Difficulty ■	Easy
Hikable ■	April to November
Length ■	2.5 miles, round trip
Fee ■	Vehicle pass
Information ■	Baldwin Ranger field office, 231-745-3100

Unmarked from the road and hidden among the towering pines of the Manistee National Forest is Bowman Lake, a beautiful body of water surrounded by forested ridges and towering pines. The lake, really a glacial depression, lies in the southern end of the Bowman Lake Foot Travel Area, a 1000-acre tract that the U.S. Forest Service calls a "semi-primitive non-motorized area."

The hilly terrain is crisscrossed by unmarked paths and split north-to-south by almost 3 miles of the North Country Trail, the national trail that will span 3200 miles from North Dakota to New York when it is completed. But circling the lake is Bowman Lake Trail, a 2.5-mile pathway that is well marked by a series of blue diamonds and easy to follow. The trail makes for a scenic but short day hike that is ideal for hikers under the age of six.

You can spend one to two hours walking the path, or pack in lunch,

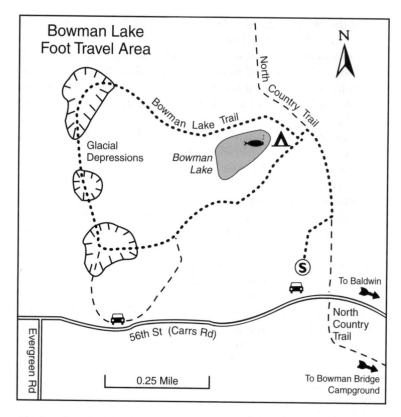

a rod and reel, and a can of worms and spend the afternoon fishing along the shoreline for panfish and bass. Bring a tent and sleeping bags and spend the night on a ridge above the lake, and chances are you might be the only ones watching the moon rise over the water.

To reach Bowman Lake from M-37 in Baldwin, head west on Seventh Street and follow it as it curves and becomes 56th Street (also labeled Carrs Road). Within 6 miles you cross the Pere Marquette River and pass the entrance to Bowman Bridge Campground. The main trailhead and parking lot for the foot travel area is 1.5 miles farther west on 56th Street. A second trailhead is another 0.5 mile farther west; if you pass the Evergreen Cemetery, you've gone too far.

A daily, weekly, or annual Huron-Manistee Recreation vehicle pass is required to park at the Bowman Lake trailhead. In Baldwin you can purchase a pass at the Baldwin Ranger field office at 650 North Michigan Avenue or at Johnson's Lodge where M-37 crosses the Pere Marquette River.

At the main trailhead a display marks the North Country Trail, where the hike begins. The North Country Trail travels along the base of a steep ridge and within 0.5 mile you reach a junction where the North Country Trail continues north, while Bowman Lake Trail heads left (west) over a low point in the ridge. Just on the other side is Bowman Lake, a serene body of water where there isn't a cottage in sight.

Bowman Lake is a glacial depression that filled in with water when the ice melted. Its shoreline of steep ridges gives you the feeling of northwoods seclusion, even though you're only a half mile from where you left the car.

At the east end are the three backcountry campsites, each basically a fire ring and a level spot to pitch a tent within full view of the lake.

The lake's muddy bottom makes swimming less than desirable, even on the hottest afternoons, but it's good for the fish. Occasionally anglers portage-in a canoe or a belly boat and then work the lake for bass, bluegill, or redear, another species of panfish. But kids can easily fish from shore, as a path edges the entire lake.

From the campsites head right (northwest) to continue along the Bowman Lake Trail as it follows the northern shore and then climbs away from the lake. It doesn't take long to reach the first of three

A young backpacker studies a map along the Bowman Lake Trail in Manistee National Forest.

glacial depressions, marked by wooden pillars in the path. Also carved by glaciers 10,000 years ago, these depressions never filled with water and today appear as large pits devoid of trees in the middle.

In the third depression is a junction, with one fork heading southwest to the second trailhead on 56th Street; the main trail continues at the east end of the depression and leads you back into the trees. It's another 0.5 mile through the forest before you descend into view of the lake again, a happy moment for young hikers who might have been doubting your navigation ability. The trail follows the south side of the lake before returning to the junction with the North Country Trail where you can backtrack to the parking area.

For more information on the North Country Trail, contact the North Country Trail Association (phone 616-454-5506).

Opposite: *Iargo Springs from the Highbanks Trail*

LAKE HURON

21

SANILAC PETROGLYPHS

Location ▪	Sanilac State Historic Site
County ▪	Sanilac
Type ▪	Interpretive walk
Difficulty ▪	Easy
Hikable ▪	April to November
Length ▪	1.5 miles
Fee ▪	None
Information ▪	Port Crescent State Park, 989-738-8663; Michigan Historical Center, 517-373-3559

Woods, a gentle stream, the possibility of encountering wildlife, and easy hiking are reasons why the trail in Sanilac State Historic Site is such a good family outing. But what makes it an excellent adventure for children is the way the historic artifacts fill young minds with images of ancient hunters, Indian villages, and nineteenth-century loggers.

The main feature of the park is a large slab of sandstone with dozens of carvings on it that archaeologists believe to be almost 1000 years old, dating back to the Late Woodland Period. They are the only petroglyphs ever found in Michigan. From the petroglyphs a 1.5-mile trail winds through the 238-acre state park unit. Numbered posts along the trail correspond to an interpretive brochure available at the park entrance.

The park is located 13 miles south of Bad Axe. From M-53, 4 miles from its junction with M-81, turn east on Bay City–Forestville Road. In 3 miles turn south on Germania Road to the posted entrance. Petroglyph signs appear on both M-53 and Bay City–Forestville Road.

From Memorial Day to Labor Day, the state Bureau of History staffs the park with interpretive guides from 11:30 A.M. to 4:30 P.M. Wednesday through Sunday. Guides assist visitors in recognizing the carvings and lead walks along the park's trail system.

From the parking lot it is a 0.25-mile walk to a large pavilion that has been built over the slab of sandstone. Most of the carvings—outlines of hands, animal tracks, birds, and spirals—are not visible at first glance. A display near the entrance shows their locations, and the best viewing is on overcast days when you can use a flashlight to illuminate the petroglyphs from the side.

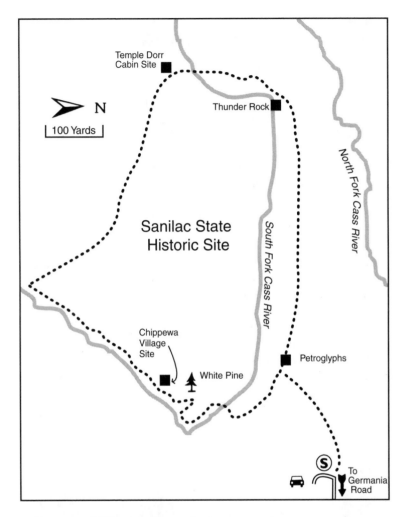

But even children can guess the most prominent one—a bowman with a long, single arm depicting both his arm and arrow—and it's fun trying to figure out what the rest could be. Deer? Hunters? Mythological creatures, maybe?

With such a great start to the walk, some young hikers head up the trail half expecting a tipi around every bend. Eight interpretive posts line the route. The first, a few steps from the rock carvings, shows where the "council circle" was located for a Chippewa tribe that once had a village here. In 0.25 mile, the second post points out some surface rocks with large, round depressions believed to be mortars that

Indians made to store and protect food. The mortars were easy to make—the Indians simply pounded the soft sandstone with round, hard rocks. Larger mortars are at Thunder Rock, the third stop.

At this point the trail curves south, close to South Fork Cass River, and passes through a lowland forest. The large maple trees arching over the river are impressive in the fall, but come spring this can be a muddy section. The moisture and mud, however, encourage a profusion of wildflowers in May and June, when the trails are crisscrossed with easy-to-identify deer tracks leading off in every direction.

In a little more than 0.5 mile from the pavilion, the trail crosses a swing bridge over the river; on the other side interpretive post number 4 marks an earthen mound that was the foundation of Temple Dorr's cabin, a timber cruiser who lived here in 1835. Just up the trail is a rock outcropping where loggers once rolled logs down into the river to float them to the Saginaw mills. The trail passes some impressive birch trees and then emerges into a semi-open area for the remainder of the hike. It was here (post number 7) that the Chippewa village was located. As late as 1900 Indians from a Caro reservation spent the summer months here while they picked and dried wild berries. If you search around, you can find more mortars.

The impressive pine nearby is a lone survivor of the Great Fire of 1881, an event that closed the chapter on logging in Michigan's Thumb region. From the towering pine (great place for a snack), you return to the river at a well-built beaver dam and then, just below the structure, cross to the other bank on another swing bridge. The pavilion is now only minutes away.

Swing bridge over the South Fork Cass River, Sanilac State Historic Site

22 HURON SAND DUNES

Location ■	Port Crescent State Park
County ■	Huron
Type ■	Day hike
Difficulty ■	Moderate
Hikable ■	April to November
Length ■	2.3 miles
Fee ■	Vehicle entry fee
Information ■	Port Crescent State Park, 989-738-8663

The sand dunes along Lake Huron can't compare in stature with those along the west side of Michigan. But to hikers with short legs and small arms, the dunes in Port Crescent State Park are soft mountains to be climbed and conquered. Parents are usually equally impressed with the sweeping panoramas that the high perches of sand provide. This excellent hike combines the dunes and good views with a woodland walk; as part of an overnight stay in the park's beachside campground, it makes for a wonderful outdoor weekend for families.

Keep in mind, however, that Port Crescent State Park is an extremely popular campground from late June through August, so it's best to book a site in advance by calling the Michigan State Parks Central Reservation System, 800-44-PARKS.

The park is located 5 miles west of Port Austin on M-25 and is split in half by the Pinnebog River, with the trail in the eastern half. One trailhead is the old iron bridge at the corner of M-25 and Port Crescent Road, providing direct access to both the blue loop (1.3 miles) and the red loop (1.1 miles). My children prefer starting at the other trailhead, located in the campground across from the modern restroom and between two beachfront sites.

From the edge of this beautiful swimming beach on Saginaw Bay, begin by kicking off your shoes and scrambling around the mouth of the Old Pinnebog River Channel. Then head toward the yellow posts, and there they are . . . the first of many small dunes of sand. If the sun is out and the temperatures warm, it's hard for children to resist the temptation of rolling down the sandy mounds.

   The short yellow spur ascends to the first scenic vista and a bench, offering views of the old river channel and the campground below. From there the blue loop begins. You can descend south along the old channel or, to hike the most impressive section of the trail first, go west through a wooded ravine.

   Heading west, you remain away from the water and sand for 0.3 mile. Keep an eye out for blue diamonds on the trees as the trail turns sharply north to return within view of the bay and more of the open dunes that border it. In another 0.25 mile you'll reach the junction of the red and blue loops, marked by a large pole and another bench. Follow the blue markers south and then north along the river channel to return to the yellow spur and reduce the walk to 1.8 miles.

   But continue west for more views. Follow the red poles and diamonds, and soon you'll emerge at another bench with a panorama of the mouth of the Pinnebog River, the Saginaw Bay shoreline, and a

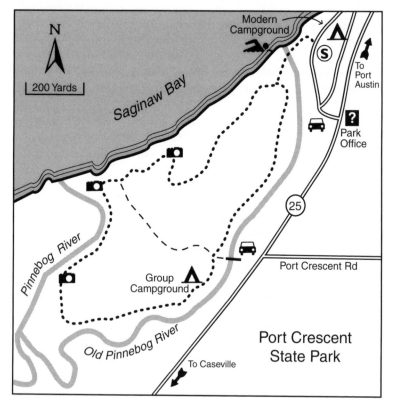

A young hiker pauses at Port Crescent State Park

stretch of open dunes. It's the best view in the park, but the steep drop of sand at your feet is what will intrigue young hikers. Wouldn't it be fun just to run down and . . . .

For the next 0.4 mile the trail continues along this sandy bluff with the river below, until it reaches one final bench where you can see much of the Pinnebog and the wetlands it flows through. At this point the trail swings south and then east, becoming a walk through woods. In another 0.4 mile you reach the group campground (vault toilets and a picnic shelter) and then the junction at the old iron bridge. Drop down toward the bridge to pick up the blue loop, which follows the old channel before climbing up to the junction with the yellow spur.

23 SHIAWASSEE WATERFOWL TRAIL

Location ■	Shiawassee National Wildlife Refuge
County ■	Saginaw
Type ■	Day hike
Difficulty ■	Moderate
Hikable ■	April to November
Length ■	5 miles
Fee ■	None
Information ■	Shiawassee National Wildlife Refuge headquarters, 989-777-5930

The Shiawassee Waterfowl Trail in the Shiawassee National Wildlife Refuge is an interesting walk almost any time of the year, as it provides dry footing through an area of marshes, ponds, and other moist soil units managed for a variety of wildlife. But during the peak migration seasons of March through April and September through early November, this day hike offers an impressive view of water-fowl, especially Canada geese.

At the height of migration, some 25,000 to 40,000 geese and 50,000 ducks gather on the refuge. From the observation tower, the halfway point of the 5-mile hike, you can watch flocks of hundreds rise in unison off the water, circle the refuge twice, and then depart. You are also sure to spot muskrats and possibly a variety of other

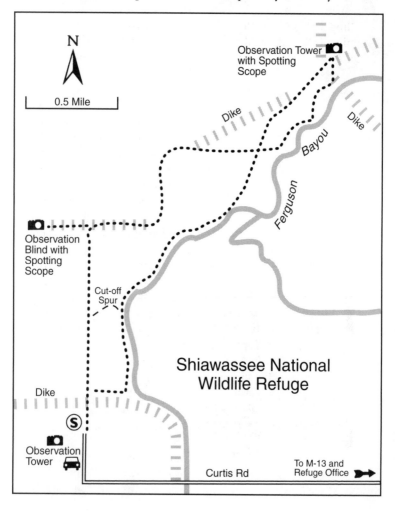

wildlife, including great blue heron, great egrets, bald eagles, or some 200 other species of birds, as well as beaver or even white-tailed deer.

The refuge is south of Saginaw and reached from I-75 by departing at exit 149 and heading west on M-46 (exit 149). Turn south on M-13 for 6 miles and then west on Curtis Road. The refuge headquarters is reached in 0.75 mile on Curtis Road and Mower Road. The headquarters is open Monday through Friday 7:00 A.M. to 4:00 P.M., but an outside information box with trail brochures is provided for weekend hikers and others. The trailhead is another 3.5 miles west at the end of Curtis Road where you turn north to reach a parking area and trail sign.

Calling it a trail is a little misleading. What you are walking on most of the time is a series of dikes that form a maze through this 9042-acre refuge. On either side of you might be a marsh, a flooded pond, a wooded area, or a field of corn planted to provide food for waterfowl. Most likely you'll see dozens of muskrats swimming in ponds or scur-

rying down the dikes, but keep a sharp eye out for ducks, other birds, turtles, or the downed trees that were gnawed by beavers.

At the parking area are interpretive displays and a tower to assist visitors in searching the surrounding fields for geese. From there the trail heads north, and within 0.5 mile is the cut-off that shortens the walk to 1.5 miles. In another 0.5 mile from the cut-off is a junction. The two-track that heads west leads to an observation blind where visitors can use a spotting scope to look for geese in the fields or flocks of mallards, green-winged teals, and black ducks on Pool 2 to the north.

Using the spotting scope at Shiawassee National Wildlife Refuge

You backtrack to the junction and follow the trail as it zigzags its way east, crosses the return trail, and then reaches Ferguson Bayou, a beautiful area of low-lying woods and marshes. (Some hikers mistakenly head left up the return trail before reaching the waterway.) The observation tower is 0.5 mile away, the halfway point and a great place for lunch. The wooden structure also features a spotting scope and provides an overview of the fields and ponds bordering the Shia-wassee River, with more crops to the west, impounded water to the northeast, and, most likely, geese everywhere. By the hundreds or even thousands they will be waddling through vegetation, floating on the surface of ponds, or running across the water in a Herculean effort to get their eight-pound bodies airborne. At peak migration, when more than 25,000 geese congregate here, the area is, as one refuge biologist said, "like O'Hare Airport at Christmas—geese are flying everywhere."

You follow a different route back from the observation tower and in 0.5 mile come to the posted junction passed earlier in the hike; continue straight. From there you're still 1.75 miles from the trailhead, with much of the walk bordering the green tree reservoir, a forest flooded each spring by meltwater runoff.

24 WITCH HAZEL TRAIL AND LUMBERJACK LOOP

Location ▪	Ringwood Forest County Park
County ▪	Saginaw
Type ▪	Interpretive walk
Difficulty ▪	Easy to moderate
Hikable ▪	April to December
Length ▪	3 miles
Fee ▪	None
Information ▪	Saginaw Parks and Recreation Commission, 989-790-5280

Ringwood Forest is an out-of-the-way and lightly developed county park bordering the South Branch Bad River. In the spring the woods can be a bit sloppy and in early summer a little buggy. But by late June the trails are dry, by mid-August most of the bugs are gone, and by late September the hardwoods are already turning colors. Arrive in October, and the forest will be a dazzling array of fall colors.

The 160-acre park features 3 miles of trails that form three basic loops, including Lumberjack Loop, an interpretive trail with numbered posts that correspond to a brochure. This is an ideal place to take young children for a hike. The trees are grand, the walking is easy, and the remote location of Ringwood Forest means families can enjoy the solitude and silence of woods even on the weekends.

To reach the park from St. Charles, head south on M-52 for 2 miles and then west on Ring Road. Within 2 miles Ring Road ends at the park entrance.

The only developed areas of the park are the canoe launch and the picnic area with tables, restrooms, and a pavilion. Head toward to the canoe launch to begin on Witch Hazel Trail. This wide path immediately crosses a bridge into the wooded floodplains of the South Branch Bad River that have been dubbed "Muskrat Flats" and then crosses the river itself via a second bridge. From there the 1.8-mile loop winds under a canopy of hardwoods before backtracking across the two bridges.

At the canoe landing you can pick up Walnut Ridge Trail, part of the second loop that leads you around the picnic area and past observations decks and benches overlooking the Bad River. At 2.2 miles into the hike you merge into Lumberjack Loop and arrive at a scenic overlook where you can gaze at the rippling waters of the Bad River.

Lumberjack Loop is a mile-long interpretive trail with 14 posts

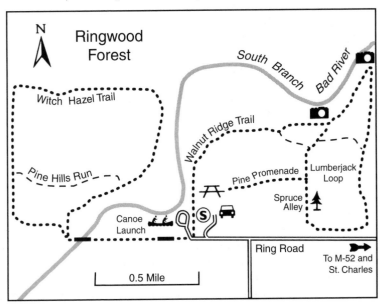

that examine both the natural history of the area and its logging past. If you follow this loop clockwise, you end with the stretch known as Spruce Alley before taking Pine Promenade Trail back to the picnic area.

Spruce Alley is the site of one of the first pine plantations to be planted in the state. William Lee Ring reforested the tract in 1883 with spruce after his father had logged off the original trees. Today this is the most impressive spot in the park, a stretch of trail where century-old pines tower above you on both sides.

25 RED PINE PATHWAY

Location ▪	Red Pine Natural Area
County ▪	Roscommon
Type ▪	Interpretive walk
Difficulty ▪	Easy
Hikable ▪	April to November
Length ▪	1.5 miles
Fee ▪	None
Information ▪	Roscommon Office, Department of Natural Resources, 989-275-5151

There was somebody else on Red Pine Pathway.

My son and I could hear movement just ahead of us, so we quietly walked around the bend, and in the middle of the trail was a covey of ruffed grouse. There were almost a dozen birds, and half of them puffed up their neck feathers as they ran across the path. When we took a step toward them the grouse exploded into the air, flying erratically between the trees.

The wildlife encounter was impressive, but we quickly returned to what we found even more fascinating: the size of the trees that towered above us. We were walking through a stand of old-growth pine, huge 200-year-old trees, with some of the white pine rivaling the trophies at Hartwick Pines State Park. But while the Hartwick Pines attract thousands of visitors every year, on this particular Sunday we were the only ones at Red Pine Natural Area.

The natural area actually covers 164 acres, but it is the 34-acre grove of virgin pines in the middle, most of them red pine, that makes the preserve so unusual. Winding through this stand of ancient trees is a 1.5-mile interpretive trail with sixteen stops and an accompanying brochure, available at the Roscommon Office, Department of Natural Resources.

To reach the preserve from I-75, take exit 222 and head north on County Road F-97 for 11 miles. Turn east (right) on Sunset Drive. Red Pine Natural Area is posted on Sunset Drive across from Kirtland Community College. At the natural area sign continue east on a dirt road, and within 0.5 mile you will arrive at the parking lot and trailhead for Red Pine Pathway.

From the parking area the trail leads east into the woods and quickly passes a large display map. Just beyond it is the first of the numbered posts and a giant red pine. This 34-acre stand of virgin red pine is typical of the forests that once covered the heart of Michigan's Lower Peninsula. The notion that this old-growth pine may have preceded the founding of our country is mind-boggling. Even my children have developed a reverence for such large specimens. These are trees you don't see in your backyard or anybody's backyard.

Within 0.4 mile the trail forks. Head right to quickly reach post number 6, which marks a dead and decaying trunk. When this tree was alive it was the "Champion of Michigan," the largest red pine in the state, measuring more than 15 feet around its trunk and standing 112 feet high.

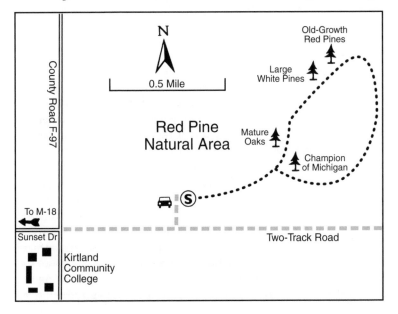

After post number 8 the trail begins to loop back, and at post number 10 there will be towering pines all around you. Stand for a moment and absorb this setting. This is what Michigan looked like back in the early 1800s when such forests covered the northern half of the state. By 1930, however, 92 percent of Michigan's old-growth forest had been cut, burned, or cleared for commercial, agricultural, or urban development.

Post number 16 points out a massive oak and scars on the base of pines that date back to forest fires in 1718, 1888, and 1928. At this point the trail returns to the intersection, where you bear right to return to the parking lot.

26 HIGHBANKS TRAIL

Location ■ Huron National Forest
County ■ Iosco
Type ■ Day hike
Difficulty ■ Moderate to challenging
Hikable ■ April to November
Length ■ 4 miles, one way
Fee ■ Vehicle pass
Information ■ Huron Shores Ranger Station, 989-739-0728; Lumberman's Monument, 989-362-8961

Strung along the towering bluffs above the AuSable River is the Highbanks Trail, a skiing and hiking route that was developed through the Corsair Ski Council and the Huron National Forest. This is a point-to-point trail, and without two vehicles, it's almost impossible to avoid backtracking. Also, the route winds close to River Road at times, and the sound of cars speeding by occasionally breaks up the peaceful tranquility of the wooded path.

But the drawbacks are hardly worth considering when compared with what the Highbanks Trail has to offer: outstanding scenery and views, the possibility of spotting bald eagles during the spring and summer, or a stop at the Lumberman's Monument to learn about the life of a logger in the 1800s. With its mostly level contour along the tops of the bluffs, this trail makes an excellent outing for children.

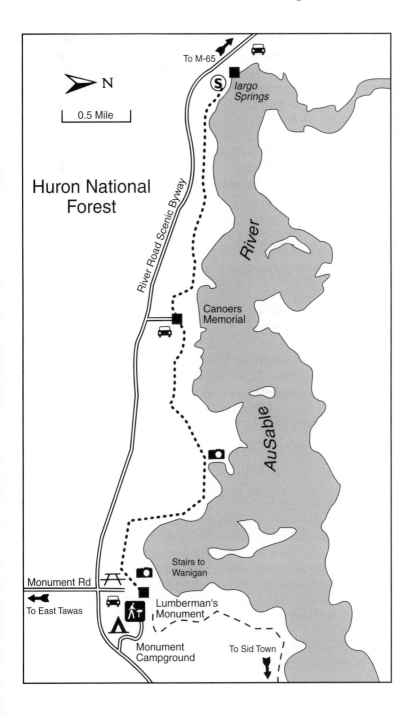

N

0.5 Mile

To M-65

Iargo
Springs

Huron National
Forest

River Road Scenic Byway

River

Canoers
Memorial

AuSable

Stairs to
Wanigan

Monument Rd

To East Tawas

Lumberman's
Monument

Monument
Campground

To Sid Town

The monuments to the past and the panoramas of the river will keep their minds off tired feet.

The entire trail, a 7-miles-one-way walk from Iargo Springs to a cluster of cottages known as Sid Town, makes for too long a day for most kids. The most interesting segment is from Iargo Springs to the Lumberman's Monument, a 4-mile trek that is much more manageable for younger hikers. You can shorten that to 2.2 miles by beginning midway at the Canoers Memorial, but Iargo Springs is an intriguing area that should not be missed.

Iargo Springs, the western trailhead for the Highbanks Trail, is a mile east of M-65 on River Road. The Lumberman's Monument, 3 miles farther east along River Road, has picnic areas, restrooms, drinking water, a campground, and a museum with hands-on exhibits and interpretive displays.

At Iargo Springs most people begin their walk with a 300-step descent to the AuSable River. At the bottom of the bluff is 0.25 mile of boardwalk that winds through towering cedars and past eight observation decks—half of them perched above the gurgling springs, the rest overlooking the AuSable.

Iargo is the Chippewa word for "many waters," and it is believed that Native Americans gathered here once for tribal pow-wows where they would drink the cold, clear water for medicinal powers. Today Iargo is still a tonic. No matter how many cars are zipping along River Road, the springs are always a quiet and tranquil spot that soothes the soul.

From the Iargo Springs parking lot, the Highbanks Trail heads east as a footpath marked by blue diamonds. You come to a powerline and follow it briefly before swinging back into the forest and arriving at your first panorama of the hike: a spectacular view of the river valley from the bluff.

The trail hugs the forested edge of the bluff, teasing you with glimpses of the AuSable River, until it breaks out at the Canoers Memorial, 1.8 miles from the start. The stone monument, topped by a pair of paddles, was originally built as a memorial to Jerry Curley, who died training for the AuSable River Canoe Marathon. Today it stands in honor of all racers who attempt the annual 150-mile event from Grayling to Oscoda, often cited as the toughest canoe race in the country.

One of the best places to catch a glimpse of an eagle along the trail is at the Canoers Memorial, where there is an active nest across the river. While the nest itself is not visible, hikers will often spot the eagles soaring high above the river beginning in April. Occasionally you can even see adult eagles returning to the nest with a steelhead trout in their talons.

Beyond the monument, the trail emerges from the woods and again follows the powerlines for 0.5 mile. Keep an eye out for the blue diamonds, but it's hard to get lost here, even when the trail takes a hard left to swing away from the lines and return to the woods. At

The Lumberman's Monument along the Highbanks Trail

3 miles from Iargo Springs you come to one the best views of the day: Standing on the edge of the bluff, you can see miles of river to the east as well as the steep banks that line the AuSable Valley.

The trail skirts the bluff for the next 0.5 mile and then passes underneath the powerlines. You return to the woods for the final 0.5 mile, a level walk through a red pine plantation, to arrive at the Lumberman's Monument.

The centerpiece of this day-use area is a 14-foot bronze statue erected in 1931 as a memorial to the lumbermen who harvested Michigan's giant white pine. The monument features three loggers: a timber cruiser with his compass, a sawyer with his cross-cut saw, and a river rat using a peavey to turn a log. Near the statue an interpretive center features exhibits devoted to the era from 1850 to 1910 when Michigan was the country's greatest wood-producing state. At one of the outdoor displays children can try their hand at using a peavey to turn a giant log.

Here also a 260-step stairway descends to the banks of the AuSable where, tied up at the bottom of the stairs, is a re-created wanigan, the cook's raft that followed the log drives and kept the river rats well fed. You can board the raft and peek inside the tent. The Lumberman's Monument is open daily from 10:00 A.M. to 5:00 P.M. from mid-May through mid-October.

27 REID LAKE

Location ■	Huron National Forest
County ■	Alcona
Type ■	Day hike or overnight
Difficulty ■	Moderate
Hikable ■	April to November
Length ■	4.2 miles
Fee ■	Vehicle pass
Information ■	Huron Shores Ranger Station, 989-739-0728; Mio Ranger District, 989-826-3252

The U.S. Forest Service manages a number of backcountry areas in Michigan's four national forests to provide a recreation experience free from the sights, sounds, and frantic pace of our motorized society. Among these foot-travel areas, Reid Lake in the Huron National Forest is one of the smallest, encompassing only 3000 acres and 6 miles of gently rolling trails.

For most people, it's a day hike into the area to view or fish the lake. But for children, the mileage is just right for an enjoyable backpacking trip, highlighted by an evening camped on the high banks above the lake or an afternoon catching panfish. Not only do the short trail distances turn Reid Lake into an excellent family backpacking trip, but the Forest Service has installed campsites, fire rings, vault toilets, and a well near the lake to make a night spent in the woods a more comfortable experience.

The foot travel area is reached from Harrisville by heading 19 miles west on M-72 to the posted entrance. From Mio, head east on M-72 21 miles to its junction with M-65 near Curran, then continue along M-72 for another 10 miles to the entrance on the south side of the state highway. A daily, weekly, or annual Huron-Manistee Recreation vehicle pass is required to park at the Reid Lake trailhead. You can purchase a pass at Huron Shores Ranger District station in Oscoda or the Mio Ranger District office.

A display board at the parking area provides maps and a box where you can post your hiking intentions. Although the trail winds around several bog areas, it is surprisingly dry and can be walked in tennis shoes. Bring a lot of bug repellent in June and July, however.

There are 6.1 miles of trails around the lake. The route described here is the most scenic loop and makes for a 2.7-mile hike to a lakeside campsite the first day and then a 1.5-mile return to the parking area. To reach the junction marked by post number 2, head left (east) at the display board along a wide trail built to accommodate both hikers and skiers. This is a trip where you can walk two abreast most of the way.

In the first mile, the trail passes through the perfect rows of a red pine plantation, moves into a hardwood forest, and ends in a stand of paper birch. From here you make a long ascent to post number 2, 1.3 miles from the start and marked by a locator map sign. Reid Lake is only 0.3 mile to the west (right), but head east for a much more interesting route.

Within minutes you arrive at one end of Mossy Bog where it's amazing to see how much plant life one fallen log can sustain. The trail curves around the bog, ascends into a stand of paper birch, and then 1.7 miles from the trailhead passes another wet area, a green-carpeted pond with a centerpiece of standing dead trees. Sure, a few

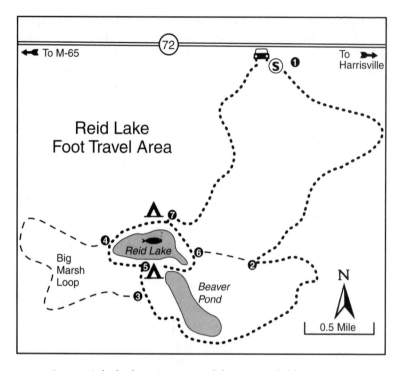

mosquitoes might be buzzing around, but even children can see there is beauty in bogs and wetlands.

The trail soon passes the rest of the bog and then ascends a low ridge to drop down to the south end of Beaver Pond, marked by an impressive beaver dam that looks for all the world like a well-laid woodpile. The trail crosses in front of the dam on planking and then skirts the rest of the pond, a body of water as big as Reid Lake. In the middle is a large lodge, while along the banks are fallen trees with the telltale signs of a beaver's handiwork—gnawed stumps and wood chips. Sit long enough on the high banks, and eventually you'll see him swim by.

From the pond the trail moves into an open field, makes two sharp, well-posted ninety-degree turns, and then arrives at post number 3. To the west (left) is Big Marsh Loop, a 1.3-mile spur around Fannies Marsh and Big Marsh. Straight to the north is Reid Lake, just one low ridge away. You quickly come to post number 5 and then swing east (right) to descend to another locator map and a "Campsites" sign. Follow this side trail to a pair of shaded sites situated on a bluff over-looking the lake.

From the campsites you can see all four fishing piers on the lake, two on the south shore and another two on the north shore. Reid is stocked annually with rainbow trout, but also holds good populations of panfish, especially bluegill. Trout are most often caught by anglers who take the time to haul in a canoe, but the panfish can be landed easily from the docks on the north side. For either fish, simple rigs of small hooks, a worm, and a couple of split shots are sufficient. Add a bobber if you're dock-fishing for bluegill.

Back at post number 5, the trail rounds the west end of the lake and in 0.25 mile comes to post number 4, the junction with the other end of Big Marsh Loop. Head up the spur to reach the well in 100 yards, or continue along the lake to pass the docks, two other campsites, and vault toilets. Lakeshore Loop ends at post number 7, where you head inland to return to the parking area. This final leg is like a road through the woods and for the most part gently descends for almost a mile to the trailhead.

28 SINKHOLES PATHWAY

Location ▪	Mackinaw State Forest
County ▪	Presque Isle
Type ▪	Day hike
Difficulty ▪	Easy to moderate
Hikable ▪	April to November
Length ▪	2.4 miles
Fee ▪	None
Information ▪	Gaylord Office, Department of Natural Resources, 989-732-3541

Kids are krazy about karsts! A karst is a limestone region of conical depressions called sinkholes, abrupt ridges, caverns, and underground streams—all of which make for interesting hiking terrain. Michigan's most visible karsts are found along the Sinkholes Pathway, a 2.4-mile loop around five such depressions, some more than 100 feet deep. If that's too much in one day for a child, there's a 0.8-mile cut-off trail that allows you to tour the first three sinkholes, which are the steepest.

Better yet, spend a weekend kamping in karstland. The Sinkhole Area is a 2600-acre tract of the Mackinaw State Forest which includes several lakes and four rustic campgrounds. A five-minute walk from the Sinkhole Pathway trailhead is Shoepac Lake State Forest Campground, with twenty-eight sites well spaced in a thick hardwood forest. None of the sites are on the water, but nearby is a small day-use area on the lake as well as a boat launch.

Our favorite campground in the area is Tomahawk Lake, which features twenty-five sites, more than half of them directly on the lake, as well as the best beach and swimming area. The choice of anglers, however, are the East Unit and West Unit campgrounds on Tomahawk Creek Flooding. The East Unit is a particularly scenic facility, as most of its twenty sites are situated on the edge of a high bluff overlooking the lake and its pair of nesting loons.

The area is located 16 miles north of Atlanta or 8 miles south of Onaway along M-33. From the state highway, turn east onto Tomahawk Lake Highway where you will pass the posted entrances to the campgrounds on Tomahawk Creek Flooding and then

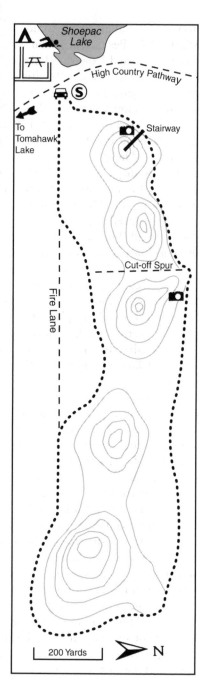

Tomahawk Lake Campground. Within 2.2 miles turn north on a dirt road posted "Shoepac Lake Campground." In a mile this road leads past the entrance of the rustic campground and then reaches a parking area within view of Shoepac Lake, which is really a sinkhole whose underground drainage was completely sealed off by clay and silt deposits, allowing it to fill with water.

The trailhead is located across the dirt road. The pathway is not difficult but does require climbing a few long slopes. Boots are not required, and most families hike the entire loop in less than two hours. From the display sign, the trail veers to the left (north) and immediately comes to the first and largest sinkhole. It's amazing how deep and steep the holes are—you can stand on the

Looking into a sinkhole along the Sinkholes Pathway in Mackinaw State Forest

edge and view the tops of trees and pines growing along the sides.

The sinkholes formed because the bedrock in this area is limestone, which dissolves easily in winter. Underground streams created large, circular caves in the limestone, which then collapsed under the overwhelming load of sand, clay, and broken rocks left behind by the last glacier 10,000 years ago.

These are dry sinkholes, unlike Shoepac Lake, and 200 yards from the trailhead you come to an observation deck. From a platform extending out over the edge of the first sinkhole, you can peer into this forested pit and then scramble down 180 steps to its floor—an unusual way to view this geological oddity, but keep in mind that it's a knee-bending climb back up, especially for young children.

From the observation platform the trail skirts the edge of the second sinkhole and then at 0.4 mile arrives at post number 2, the junction of the cut-off loop. Head right (south) to return to the parking area or straight ahead (east) to hike the entire pathway. If you continue east, you'll soon reach the third hole. This karst also

CAUTION

features an observation deck but not a stairway to the bottom.

You then swing away to cross an area of scattered pines, the result of a 1939 forest fire. You pass a view of the fourth hole at 0.8 mile and then cut through more regenerating forest before coming to post number 3. At this point the trail swings south and makes a long ascent through a pine plantation to top off in a thick growth of aspen.

At 1.3 miles the trail swings west to give way to the only view of the fifth sinkhole. You move from aspen to the jack pine that took root after the 1939 fire, and at 1.7 miles pass the south edge of the fourth hole.

The trail swings inland at this point, but many parties unwittingly continue on the arrow-straight track, which is a fire lane. At 2 miles you reach post number 4, the junction with the cut-off spur, and then finish the hike by rounding the south side of the first two holes and viewing the sandy edge on the other side where you were hiking just an hour or two earlier.

Throughout much of the last half mile of the pathway you can look down the straight trail and see the shimmering waters of Shoepac Lake. If the day is hot, it's hard to resist the temptation of dashing from the end of the pathway into the cooling waters of this most refreshing sinkhole.

29 OCQUEOC FALLS PATHWAY

Location ■ Mackinaw State Forest
County ■ Presque Isle
Type ■ Day hike
Difficulty ■ Moderate
Hikable ■ April to November
Length ■ 3 miles
Fee ■ None
Information ■ Gaylord Office, Department of Natural Resources, 989-732-3541

While the Upper Peninsula has hundreds of waterfalls, the Lower Peninsula has only two, with Ocqueoc Falls being the most popular and accessible one south of the Mackinac Bridge. You can rush from the parking lot to the falls in a couple of minutes, but the best way to turn this stop into an adventure is first to hike a portion of the Ocqueoc

Falls Pathway, a bicentennial project built in 1976. The trail is shared by hikers and mountain bikers during the summer and consists of 3-, 5-, and 6-mile loops. The pathway makes an excellent choice for children because the first and shortest loop is also the most scenic.

The trailhead is well posted on Ocqueoc Falls Road, which can be reached from Rogers City by following M-68 west for 11.5 miles. When the state highway curves sharply to the south, continue straight onto Ocqueoc Falls Road for a couple hundred yards to the entrance. Across the road from the trailhead is Ocqueoc Falls Campground, a rustic facility (hand pump, vault toilets) with many sites situated on a high bank overlooking the Ocqueoc River.

The trailhead is marked with a large display map, and immediately you have a choice to make: left or right? By heading east

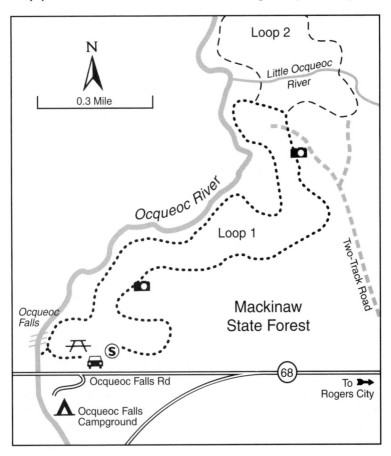

Ocqueoc Falls, one of two natural waterfalls in the Lower Peninsula

(right), you will save the most scenic section of the hike for the second half and the falls for the end. But the first leg isn't without its views either.

You begin by passing through a red pine plantation along a wide, sandy path covered with pine needles. It stays close to M-68 at first, but quickly swings away, ascending a ridge until at 0.5 mile it breaks out onto the edge, where you can look down into the river valley or across to the forested ridge bordering it on the other side. The first leg continues as a level walk along the ridge, but keep an eye out for the blue blazes on the trees to avoid wandering off on an old off-road-vehicle (ORV) trail. Just before post number 2, the trees open up briefly for the best overview of the river valley.

The junction is marked by a locator map. To extend the hike to a 5-mile walk, you can continue north (straight ahead) and follow the second loop. To stay on the first loop, head west (left), making a quick descent and coming to post number 5. Then turn south, cutting through a stump-riddled meadow and crossing a trickle of a creek in a low-lying area. From there blue blazes direct you to make a wide, ninety-degree turn west, where the trail descends right to the riverbank for the first time.

At this scenic spot (lunch, maybe?) the river's current twists and turns five times as it flows through a horseshoe bend. The trail continues south along the riverbank for the next quarter mile and, if the day is hot, it's hard to resist jumping in right here. Tell your hikers a better pool awaits them. About halfway along the leg back to the parking area, the trail climbs a high bank above the river and soon you come to another overview, 20 feet above a ∪-shaped bend in the river.

There's something about a northwoods stream gurgling past you that soothes the soul and washes the worries away. But you don't have to admire it too long from this spot, because the trail follows the river for the next 0.5 mile in what has to be one of the most beautiful stretches of stream-side hiking in Michigan. Within a quarter mile of the end, the trail veers away from the Ocqueoc and comes to a V junction. The fork to the left goes to the trailhead and display map. The one to the right leads straight to the falls, where young hikers can sit in a pool and let the cascade gush over them after their "long hike."

Ahhhhh!

30   BELL TOWNSITE

Location	▪	Besser Natural Area
County	▪	Presque Isle
Type	▪	Day hike
Difficulty	▪	Easy
Hikable	▪	April to November
Length	▪	1 mile
Fee	▪	None
Information	▪	Gaylord Office, Department of Natural Resources, 989-732-3541

What could be more exciting than viewing a shipwreck? Hiking through a ghost town, maybe? At Besser Natural Area it doesn't matter, for children are treated to both on the easy, mile-long hike through a rare stand of virgin pine.

Jesse Besser was an industrialist and founder of a massive concrete block corporation in Alpena, but in 1966 he gave to the people of Michigan a 135-acre tract of land on Lake Huron, containing a magnificent stand of virgin red and white pine that escaped the swinging axes of lumbermen in the 1800s. The preserve also contains more than a mile of Lake Huron shoreline, including a small cove with a wide, sandy beach lined by towering pines.

The somewhat remote natural area is a 20-minute drive north of Alpena and reached by departing US-23 east onto Rayburn Road and following it 1.8 miles to the posted entrance. The trailhead includes a parking area, vault toilet, and a large display map, but no drinking water.

The hike is along a path through the pines, carpeted in needles and easily hiked in tennis shoes. The first half of the trail stays close to the Lake Huron shoreline and within 0.3 mile comes to a small lagoon that contains the shipwreck. The best way to see the vessel is to slip on a pair of polarized sunglasses and leave the trail to walk along the narrow, rocky strip that encloses the pond on the east side. From here the wreck is less than 4 feet away; in the middle of the lagoon is what appears to be a gunwale.

The ship was docked at Bell, a lumbering and mill town located here in the 1800s, when it sank during a fierce storm. The vessel was never raised. After the town was abandoned, the water level of Lake Huron dropped, turning the small harbor into a lagoon with a shipwreck.

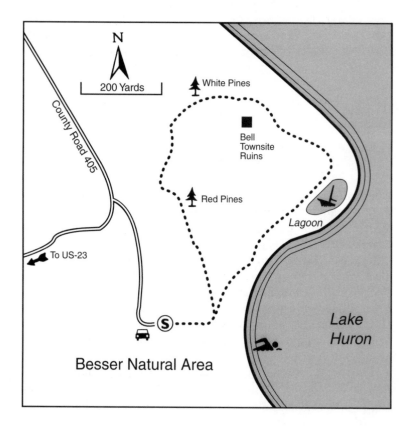

The remains of a home in the "ghost town" of Bell, as seen in Besser Natural Area

At its heyday, Bell had a population of more than 100 and contained several homes, a sawmill, a saloon, a store, and a school. The most noticeable remains of this "ghost town" are the rock pier along Lake Huron (not visible from the trail), a towering stone chimney, and the collapsed walls of a building whose steel safe and icebox counter indicate it might have been the saloon.

The trail ends by winding through some of the oldest and largest white pines remaining in a state that was once covered with them. There are also some red and Norway pines along the path, all so stately and tall that young necks strain to see the arched boughs at the tops. Plan on 20 to 30 minutes to walk the trail or, better yet, make it an afternoon adventure by bringing lunch and swimsuits for enjoying the beach.

31 NORTH BAY TRAIL

Location ■	Presque Isle Township Lighthouse Park
County ■	Presque Isle
Type ■	Day hike
Difficulty ■	Easy
Hikable ■	April to November
Length ■	1.3 miles
Fee ■	Fee to climb tower
Information ■	Lighthouse Gift Shop, 989-595-9919

There's an old legend about the New Presque Isle Lighthouse, which really isn't so new at all, having been built in 1870: According to the folktale, the wife of one keeper could not cope with the long periods of isolation and loneliness and eventually went insane. The poor husband, not knowing what to do, simply locked her up in the cellar and then bricked her in. To this day, locals will tell you, with a sly grin and a shake of the head, that on the windy nights that frequent the North Point of Presque Isle, you can still hear the woman moaning from her perpetual loneliness.

Lighthouses are always intriguing to children. But throw in a ghastly legend with a scenic but short day hike, a climb to the top of the tower, and a picnic at the end of a point, and it makes a great adventure for upstart hikers, even those as young as three.

The 99-acre township park is reached from US-23, north of Alpena, by turning onto Grand Lake Road (also called County Road 405). Follow the winding road through the town of Presque Isle, around Presque Isle Harbor, and past the old lighthouse, now a museum. The road ends at the park, which is open daily from 8:00 A.M. to 10:00 P.M.

North Bay Trail begins just north of the tower and is posted. This is a wide wood-chip path that weaves among the cedars for 0.3 mile until it arrives at the rocky limestone shoreline of North Bay. At a "North Point" sign you dip back into the cool, shaded world of a cedar forest.

New Presque Isle Lighthouse

The trail here skirts the shoreline but stays just inside the cedars. You can tell the topsoil is thin here; the trees are tilted and twisted as if you were walking through the middle of a giant game of pick-up sticks. The precarious positions of the trunks plus the gnarly nature of the cedars had my son thinking he was in the haunted forest of the Wizard of Oz; he was half expecting a branch to come down and whack him at any minute.

Every so often a spur leads out to the rocky beach and a bench. Within 0.75 mile from the trailhead you break out at North

Point. This was the site of a foghorn signal building that was built in 1890 and housed a 10-inch, steam-operated whistle. The building was removed in 1968, and today there is a pavilion with picnic tables in its place. Near the tip of the point are benches where tired hikers can rest and watch lake freighters slowly making their way across Lake Huron.

Across from the picnic shelters is the final leg of the hike, a wood-chip path posted "Nature Trail." The path stays in the forest, away from the shoreline, but the last section is lined with scenic white paper birches. It ends on a gravel road within view of the lighthouse.

There is no better way to end the hike than with a climb to the top of the tower. Built to replace Old Presque Isle Lighthouse, the coni-cal brick tower is 113 feet high, making it the tallest lighthouse struc-turally on the Great Lakes. From the attached keeper's house, which is presently a gift shop, a spiral staircase of 144 steps leads to the light at the top that was automated by the U.S. Coast Guard in 1970. Once at the top, you can step outside to the narrow balcony that encircles the tower and enjoy a stunning 360-degree view of Lake Huron and Presque Isle.

The gift shop and the tower are open during the summer from 9:00 A.M. to 6:00 P.M. There is a small fee to climb the tower. The second lightkeeper's house in the park, presently being restored as a museum, is open weekends in July and August.

32 BEAVER POND TRAIL

Location ■	Historic Mill Creek State Park
County ■	Cheboygan
Type ■	Interpretive walk
Difficulty ■	Moderate
Hikable ■	April to November
Length ■	2 miles
Fee ■	Entry fee
Information ■	Mackinac State Historic Parks, 231-436-4100

Children love Mackinac Island State Park and Colonial Michili-mackinac in Mackinaw City because of the forts, period-dressed

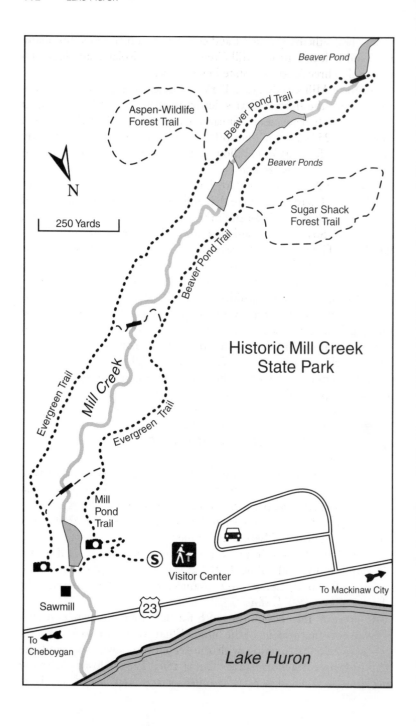

soldiers, and the daily musket and cannon demonstrations. But many never make it to Historic Mill Creek, the most isolated and least visited of the three Mackinac State Historic Parks.

Historic Mill Creek State Park is located just a few miles away from where the fleet of ferries depart for Mackinac Island, but you won't find a stockade here—or cannons or a slab of cherry nut fudge. What the 625-acre park does offer is a history of its own, few if any crowds, and footpaths that allow you to end any visit with a hike in the woods.

Settled in the 1780s, Mill Creek was one of the first industrial sites in the Great Lakes. It was here that Scotsman Robert Campbell found the only creek at the tip of the mitt with enough current to power a waterwheel. So he constructed a sawmill and made a living cutting lumber. Most of it went to the British who were in the process of abandoning Fort Michilimackinac for a new military stockade they were building on Mackinac Island.

Today period-dressed guides give lively demonstrations at a saw pit and in the reconstructed water-powered sawmill. Surrounding the building is a natural area with 3.5 miles of trails that wind through the woods, along Mill Creek, and past beaver dams and lodges.

To reach the park, leave I-75 at exit 337 in Mackinaw City and head east 3 miles on US-23. The visitor center and interpretive programs are open daily from early May to early October.

This hike makes a loop of three of the park's five trails: Mill Pond Trail, Evergreen Trail, and Beaver Pond Trail. The 2-mile loop follows one side of Mill Creek and then crosses the stream to return along the other.

You begin outside the visitor center on Mill Pond Trail, a paved path that immediately climbs the limestone bluff to an overlook. From the observation platform you can gaze over the shoreline trees to Mackinac Island and see perched on its limestone bluffs Fort Mackinac, built with Mill Creek lumber.

From here the trail heads south into the mixed forest, following the bluffs above Mill Creek. In 0.2 mile you reach a junction: to the left is the first of three crossovers to the east side of the creek; straight ahead is Evergreen Trail.

Evergreen Trail continues south for 0.25 mile but swings southwest away from the edge of the bluff. When you return to Mill Creek you arrive at the junction with the second crossover spur and the start of Beaver Pond Trail. True to its name, this trail leads you to the first beaver dam and pond 0.75 mile from the trailhead. Here is an

Visitors listen to an interpretive guide at Historic Mill Creek State Park.

interpretive display devoted to beavers, and you can gaze down at the pond from the edge of the bluff. Also nearby is the junction to Sugar Shack Forest Trail.

Beaver Pond Trail continues southwest and in another 0.25 mile descends to cross Mill Creek on a footbridge. After ascending the east-side bluffs you head north and arrive at an observation area. This one, overlooking a second beaver pond and dam, features a bench and more interpretive displays. Sit for awhile with the kids, and see if the pond's residents appear.

From the overlook, Beaver Pond Trail soon passes the junction to Aspen-Wildlife Forest Trail and then merges into Evergreen Trail. You are now 0.5 mile from the end of the hike. Along the way you pass more interpretive displays and one final observation area along Mill Pond Trail.

To lengthen the hike you can include the Sugar Shack Forest Trail (a 0.75-mile loop) or the Aspen-Wildlife Forest Trail (a 0.5-mile loop). Both trails are level walks in the woods.

Opposite: Point Sable Lighthouse in Ludington State Park

LAKE MICHIGAN

33 NIPISSING DUNE TRAILS

Location ■	Cook Energy Information Center
County ■	Berrien
Type ■	Interpretive walk
Difficulty ■	Moderate to challenging
Hikable ■	March to January
Length ■	3 miles
Fee ■	None
Information ■	Cook Energy Information Center, 800-548-2555

There were two barriers that always stopped us from hiking the Nipissing Dune Trails. The first was driving past the twin domes of a nuclear reactor. The idea of visiting the Cook Nuclear Plant to enjoy a nature hike seemed like an oxymoron ("Should we pack flashlights, Dad? Or will we just glow in the dark?"). The second was the Cook Energy Information Center, an on-site interpretive center with enough atom-splitting displays and hands-on exhibits to keep most children entertained for the afternoon. When we finally hiked the trails, my children and I decided we should have ignored those domes and passed up the center's computer games a long time ago.

As a way to demonstrate how clean and compatible nuclear power can be, the Cook Energy Information Center built the Nipissing Dune Trails, a three-loop system in 10 acres of wooded dunes bordering the nuclear plant complex. Like most trails in west Michigan's dune country, there is considerable climbing here, and families with children under the age of six might want to limit themselves to the first two loops: the Overlook Trail and Nipissing Dune Trail, both under a mile in length.

But for everybody else, the entire system makes for an enjoyable 3-mile hike where hand-hewn steps and thick ropes assist you on the steepest climbs and more than two dozen interpretive posts correspond to a brochure available at the trailhead. The brochure is a necessity, because the range of habitats this trail passes through is amazing.

 To reach Cook Energy Information Center from I-94, take exit 23 and head south on Red Arrow Highway for 3 miles. The entrance is off Red Arrow Highway just north of Bridgman, and the trailhead is in back of the parking lot.

The visitor center is open Tuesday through Sunday from 10:00 A.M. to 5:00 P.M.

From the trailhead the first loop, the Overlook Trail, immediately descends into a coastal forest of elm, maple, and white ash. Then the trail emerges in a grassy meadow, passes a dune blowout that has been sculptured by the wind, and arrives at an observation deck overlooking Lake Michigan. All this, and you've only walked 0.25 mile. This is the kind of trail kids love.

From the observation deck, the Overlook Trail quickly reaches a junction, where you head right to continue on Nipissing Dune Trail. Within a 0.25 mile you head left at the next junction to continue on the Wetland Trail. The bulk of this hike is along the Wetland Trail, which leaves the fore dunes along Lake Michigan and heads a mile inland.

This is where you appreciate those ropes the most. You grip them to haul yourself up to the top of a narrow-crested dune or when descending its backside into a hollow filled with trillium, hepatica, and the lacy white blossoms of flowering dogwood in the spring and early summer.

The up-and-down walking through the dunes ends within a mile of the trailhead, and 0.25 mile later you're following planking that weaves through an extensive interdunal wetland. The boardwalk extends for more than 0.25 mile and is one of the most impressive marsh trails in the state. You never worry about getting your socks wet while listening to spring peepers, enjoying the yellow profusion of marsh marigolds, and watching handfuls of mallards explode into the air.

The planking and the Wetland Trail end 1.5 miles from the trailhead at a massive staircase. You can either take the stairs to return to the Cook Information Center via the entrance drive or double back along the trail.

34 MUD LAKE BOG

Location ■	Mud Lake Bog Nature Preserve
County ■	Berrien
Type ■	Day hike
Difficulty ■	Easy
Hikable ■	March to January
Length ■	I mile
Fee ■	None
Information ■	Fernwood Nature Center, 616-695-6491

The sign said "Stay on the Boardwalk—No Exceptions!" So we did. But bogs are far too interesting not to get down on your knees and examine them closely. Our feet stayed on the wooden planks,

Pitcher plants growing in a bog

but our hands reached out and pushed against the mat of grasses and sedges, and a pool of water appeared.

We touched the smooth, thick sides of dormant pitcher plants which in the fall had turned cranberry red. We studied a deer trail as it weaved through the grass, crossed the boardwalk, and disappeared into the shrubs. We saw a beaver lodge but no activity.

Mud Lake Bog is an amazing little spot. Especially when you consider it was a dump twenty years ago—a haven for bed springs and beer cans, not wildlife. That's when the Township of Buchanan identified the area as an unusual ecosystem, a floating mat bog, typical of the Upper Peninsula and Canada but located only 5 miles from Indiana. In 1980, the city purchased 106 acres and then invited the staffs of nearby Fernwood and Love Creek Nature Centers to help clean up the area and turn it into a new preserve. Mud Lake Bog now features a mile of trail, most of it boardwalk, along with a picnic shelter and an observation tower.

To reach Mud Lake Bog from US-33, head west on US-12 for 7 miles and then north on Bakertown Road for 2 miles. Turn west on Elm Lake Road, and you'll reach the posted entrance of the preserve in 2.5 miles. The park is open from 7:00 A.M. to 8:00 P.M. daily. Twice a year, in the spring and fall, Fernwood Nature Center sponsors an open house at Mud Lake Bog with naturalist-led tours of the area. Call the center for exact dates.

A short trail system, which includes 0.75 mile of boardwalk, departs from the parking area and leads through the progressive stages of this dying lake. First you enter a forest of saplings and then pass through a waist-high grove of leatherleaf and other shrubs. Finally you emerge at the mat of grasses and sphagnum moss where the boardwalk is suspended on floating barrels.

Here in the middle of Mud Lake Bog hundreds of pitcher plants, my children's favorite bug-eating flora, will surround you. The boardwalk winds through the open area of the bog and then circles back to the parking area where there is a picnic shelter and an observation tower.

The tower puts you above the emerging forest and allows you to see what's actually left of Mud Lake. What was a thriving lake 10,000 years ago after the glaciers departed, is now a small patch of open water with a beaver lodge at one end. Eventually—in another thousand years or so—the plants will work their way out and cover the lake completely.

Better hurry if you want to see Mud Lake.

35 CREEK AND TRILLIUM TRAILS

Location ■	Love Creek County Park
County ■	Berrien
Type ■	Day hike
Difficulty ■	Moderate
Hikable ■	March to December
Length ■	2.8 miles
Fee ■	Vehicle entry fee
Information ■	Love Creek Nature Center, 616-471-2617

In the late 1800s Berrien County acquired acreage bordering Love Creek and set up a poor farm, a refuge where persons and families down on their luck could find work, a meal, and a temporary home. Most of the area was cleared for cultivation, but the ravine that the stream had cut was too steep and rugged to farm, so the trees that filled it were never cut.

Poor farm, priceless forest. Small pockets of rare, century-old timber survived long after the farm was gone, and in 1976 Love Creek was dedicated a natural area. The 150-acre park has six trails that total almost 5 miles. The longest loops, Creek Trail and Trillium Trail, can easily be combined for a 2.5-mile walk, with most of the hike spent among the tall timber in and near the ravine. Adding the short Marsh Ridge Trail lengthens the walk to 2.8 miles and increases your chances of spotting wildlife.

The best time to explore this area is spring and fall. In May the park is host to extensive beds of woodland flowers, particularly

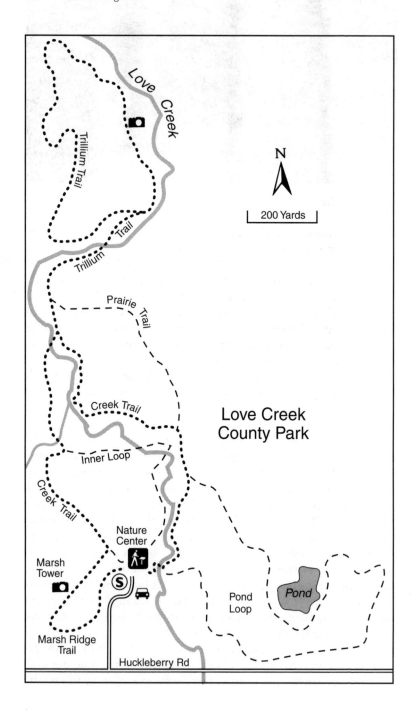

N

200 Yards

Love Creek

Trillium Trail

Trillium Trail

Prairie Trail

Creek Trail

Love Creek
County Park

Inner Loop

Creek Trail

Nature
Center

Marsh
Tower

Pond
Loop

Pond

Marsh Ridge
Trail

Huckleberry Rd

Hiker in Love Creek County Park

trillium. In fall the beech-maple forest holds its brilliant colors late into the year, often until the end of October or even longer.

To reach Love Creek from US-31, exit on Old US-31 and follow it through the town of Berrien Springs. Just after crossing the St. Joseph River, turn left onto Dean's Hill Road and then make an immediate right on Pokagon Road. Within 2 miles turn left on Huckleberry Road and follow signs to the park entrance. Love Creek is open from dawn to dusk daily, and the nature center from 10:00 A.M. to 5:00 P.M. Tuesday through Sunday.

Most of the trails depart from the nature center, including Marsh Ridge Trail. This 0.3-mile loop begins along a wooded ridge and then makes a sharp descent via a stairway. You bottom out at a wildlife observation tower overlooking a small marsh.

From the tower the trail soon merges into Creek Trail at a well-marked junction; head left (northwest). Creek Trail begins in a young successional forest, but within 0.25 mile you descend another stairway, cross a small creek, and then climb out of the ravine past towering timber. You dip down to cross Love Creek and ascend to the junction where Prairie Trail and Creek Trail meet Trillium Trail, 1 mile into the hike. Trillium Trail is the park's back loop where the maples and American beech are the tallest and fall lingers the longest.

Continuing northwest from this junction on Trillium Trail, you descend to recross Love Creek and then climb to the most interesting stretch of the day. For the next 0.5 mile the trail skirts the edge of the ravine, allowing you to look down through the foliage at Love Creek gurgling its way to the St. Joseph River.

Trillium Trail loops around to the west, and from here you retrace your steps across Love Creek and return to the junction with Creek Trail. This time, head left at the intersection to follow the northern half of the Creek Trail loop back to the nature center. This section of Creek Trail remains close to the stream and finally crosses it at the end. You're faced with one more climb before emerging at the nature center.

36 BIG TREE AND WEST LOOPS

Location ▪	Fred Russ Forest Park
County ▪	Cass
Type ▪	Day hike
Difficulty ▪	Moderate
Hikable ▪	March to December
Length ▪	3.2 miles
Fee ▪	None
Information ▪	Cass County Road Commission, 616-445-8611

While standing on a bridge in Fred Russ Forest Park, my son and I saw a small ring suddenly appear on the surface of a stream . . . and then another and another and another. Michael instinctively glanced at the sky, but there were no clouds, so it couldn't be rain. At that point he turned to me with a puzzled look.

"Trout," I said quietly. "They're feeding on insects floating along on the creek."

My five-year-old thought this was rather remarkable, that something he could only imagine happening to his worm and hook when fishing in a lake, he now could clearly see: fish feeding. What was really remarkable wasn't so much the trout but where they were rising. We were neither on the AuSable River nor even in northern Michigan, but in Cass County, about as far south as you can drive in this state.

Located on a rural road between Dowagiac and Marcellus, Fred Russ is a 10-acre Cass County park surrounded by Michigan State University's 580-acre Russ Forest Research Station. The entire area is laced by more than 4 miles of foot trails, while gently flowing through the middle of it is Dowagiac Creek, a stream highly regarded among anglers for brown trout.

By combining Big Tree Loop and West Loop, you can enjoy a moderately easy walk of 3.2 miles that includes seeing the remnants of a giant tulip tree and, depending on the season, possibly even a trout or two rising to an insect hatch. You can shorten the hike to just 1.6 miles by hiking only Big Tree Loop or West Loop.

You reach the park from M-60, 2 miles east of Cassopolis. Turn north on Decatur Road and in 6 miles left (east) on Marcellus Highway. The park entrance is posted just to the east on Marcellus Highway.

At one time the park was part of a farm, and a huge red barn still stands near the parking lot. Nearby is a display containing a third of what was once the largest tulip tree in Michigan. Known simply as the "Big Tree," it was 200 feet tall with a girth of 23.6 feet when a

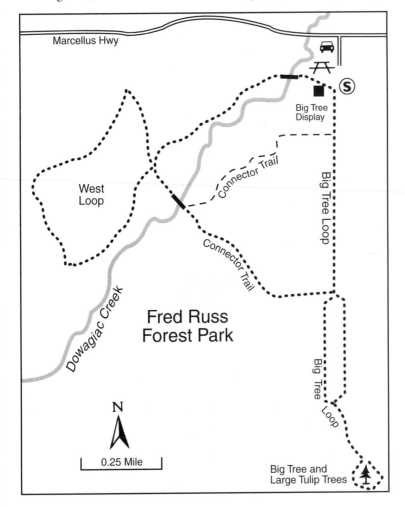

violent storm blew it down in 1984. Big Tree Loop leads due south out to the rest of the trunk and its massive stump.

The trail begins as a sandy path that is usually marred by deer prints made by white-tails traveling from the forest on one side of you to the cornfield on the other. You will also pass benches along the way and signs that point out stands of Austrian pine, black walnut, white ash, and other plantings by MSU foresters.

You pass a junction with a connector trail to West Loop and then, in less than a mile from the parking lot, arrive at a bench overlooking the Big Tree. It may be lying on the ground in several pieces, but it's still an impressive piece of lumber. It's not hard to imagine what it looked like stretched out to the sky at the end of its 300-year life. Nearby is another towering tulip tree that somehow survived the storm and still forces you to look up.

You backtrack 0.4 mile of Big Tree Loop and then head left (west) on the connector trail to West Loop. Within 0.5 mile (1.7 miles into the hike) you reach the first of two bridges across Dowagiac Creek. On the west side of the stream West Loop makes a 1-mile loop through the forest and then heads east for the parking area along Dowagiac Creek. Just before returning to the trailhead you cross the creek a second time on a bridge with benches built in the center. Here you can sit quietly and study the trout stream in front of you. If it's late in the day and your timing is right, somebody might even think it's starting to rain.

37 MOUNT BALDHEAD

Location ■	Mount Baldhead and Oval Beach Recreation Area
County ■	Allegan
Type ■	Day hike
Difficulty ■	Moderate
Hikable ■	June to September
Length ■	1 to 1.8 miles, round trip
Fee ■	Ferry passage fee
Information ■	City of Saugatuck, 616-857-2603

Saugatuck, that trendy resort town on Lake Michigan, is hardly wilderness, but it does offer a fun adventure that includes a ride on a

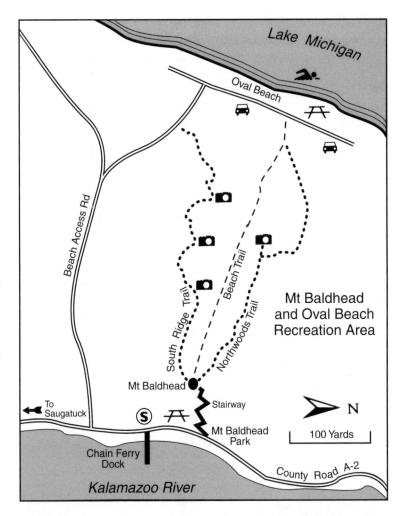

hand-pulled chain ferry, a climb up Mount Baldhead, and sweeping views from the top of the forested sand dune. It ends with a pleasant descent of the dune's west side to Oval Beach, Saugatuck's renowned stretch of sand and Lake Michigan surf.

The hike to the beach is short but does involve a stairway of 282 steps, a climb that leaves most people, parents and kids alike, puffing at the top. Benches have been built into the sides of the stairs, allowing you to take as much time and as many breaks as necessary to scale the "mountain." Pack along lunch or a snack, bathing suits, a towel, and sunscreen.

Saugatuck is south of Holland and reached by exiting onto Blue

Star Highway (A-2) from I-96. Moored along the Kalamazoo River on the edge of the town's famed shopping district is an armada of cabin cruisers and sailboats 30, 40, and 50 or more feet in length. They arrive from home ports all over the Midwest and bob impressively in their slips during the summer tourist season.

A boardwalk paralleling Water Street winds past the luxury boats and ends at the most unusual vessel afloat—the Saugatuck Chain Ferry. The unique craft is at the foot of Mary and Water Streets and is owned by the City of Saugatuck, which claims it is "the only hand-cranked chain-powered ferry on the Great Lakes," even though it only crosses the Kalamazoo River.

Saugatuck's chain ferry is a 150-year tradition. When the original one, a chain-pulled wooden barge, was put into service in 1838, it was a much-heralded event. Before then, friends and farmers spent a half day traveling 10 miles inland to a bridge in New Richmond, just to reach Douglas, which was only 100 yards across the river.

The tradition stayed alive even after the Saugatuck–Douglas bridge was completed in the 1920s. In 1965, the present ferry was built, a small barge with white gingerbread siding and a 380-foot chain to pull it through the water. The chain ferry (for foot traffic only) operates daily from the second weekend in June through Labor Day, and the trip lasts a mere 15 to 20 minutes, delivering passengers just south of Mount Baldhead Park.

The park has picnic tables, restrooms, a pavilion, and a 282-step stairway that leads to the top of the 650-foot-high sand dune. It's an invigorating climb to the top, and the view is excellent. From observation decks you can see much of downtown Saugatuck, the boat traf-

View of Saugatuck from Mount Baldhead

fic on the Kalamazoo River, even the *S.S. Keewatin*, the historic cruise liner docked in Douglas.

On the west side of the dune are three trails leading to Oval Beach. Thrill seekers choose the Beach Trail, a wild romp down a steep, sandy slope that is usually topped off by continuing across the beach and straight into the lake for a cooling dip. To the right is the posted Northwoods Trail, a 2112-foot-long path along the dune's wooded north side. This trail, with the mildest grade, passes one observation point along the way. Hiked both ways, it would make for a 1-mile round trip to the beach. Better yet to take the most scenic route to the beach, South Ridge Trail, and return on Northwoods Trail, the easiest way to ascend the sand dune, for a 1.8-mile loop

The 1534-foot-long South Ridge Trail leaves the top of the dune to the left and passes a handful of overlooks with views of Lake Michigan, Oval Beach, and Oxbow Lagoon to the north. The path makes a more rapid descent through a pine forest to emerge just south of the beach along the entrance drive. Enjoy the sand and surf. When you're ready to return, reclimb Mount Baldhead along Northwoods Trail.

38   DUNE RIDGE TRAIL

Location ■	Kirk Park
County ■	Ottawa
Type ■	Day hike
Difficulty ■	Easy
Hikable ■	March to January
Length ■	1 mile
Fee ■	Vehicle entry fee
Information ■	Ottawa County Parks and Recreation Commission, 616-738-4810

There is a tendency at Kirk Park for children to head straight to the beach. They jump out of the car and hightail it down a paved path to Lake Michigan where they jump into the surf, roll in the sand, or get scorched by the sun. Then their parents take them home, usually waterlogged, sunburnt, and with half a dune in their bathing suits.

Should have taken them hiking.

At 66 acres and with 2000 feet of lakefront, this Ottawa County park is not large. In fact, it's basically one dune. But it's a large dune, and major renovations in the mid-1990s resulted in an intriguing 2-mile trail system over and around this towering hill of sand. The heart of the system is Dune Ridge Trail, a mile-long loop that climbs the hill and then circles the top to reward hikers with excellent views of Lake Michigan.

 The park is halfway between Holland and Grand Haven. From US-31, 9 miles north of Holland, exit at Stanton Street and head west. Follow park signs to the entrance on Lakeshore Drive.

The trailhead for the system is just south of the parking lots. From here the trail continues south and in the beginning is flat as it skirts the forested base of the dune. Within 0.25 mile you arrive at a junction marked by post number 2. Head right and start climbing.

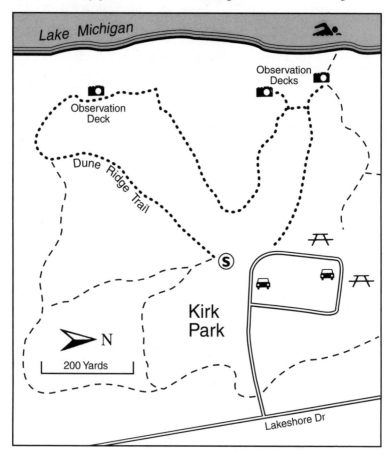

In the beginning the climb is a laborious ascent through soft sand, but the trail soon levels out and children can take a breather to peer at Lake Michigan far below. The climb resumes as a stairway. When you reach the top you're almost a 149 feet above Lake Michigan at an observation deck that provides an extended view of the shoreline below.

The trail descends from the deck via another stairway and then gently climbs along the crest of the dune. At 0.5 mile from the trailhead you reach the highest point of the park at 730 feet or almost 250 feet above the lake. You're high enough to see the interior of the park to the east, the watery horizon of Lake Michigan to the west, and Grand Haven to the north.

After a steep descent, the trail climbs once more to the third and final overlook, a deck perched at 640 feet. The descent off the dune is a long stairway where at the bottom you can head left (west) to the beach and an interpretive display that explains the delicate nature of dunes. Head east, and the trail will skirt the base of the dune and return the trailhead in 0.25 mile.

 ## DUNE CLIMB STAIRWAY

Location ■	P. J. Hoffmaster State Park
County ■	Muskegon
Type ■	Day hike
Difficulty ■	Easy
Hikable ■	March to December
Length ■	1 mile, round trip
Fee ■	Vehicle entry fee
Information ■	P. J. Hoffmaster State Park headquarters, 231-798-3711; Gillette Visitor Center, 231-798-3573

You can view the most famous dunes in the Midwest all along the state's Lake Michigan shoreline, but the best place to teach children the significance of these mountains of sand is at P. J. Hoffmaster State Park on the outskirts of the city of Muskegon. An afternoon in the park with young children, even those under the age of five or six, can begin with a visit to Gillette Visitor Center to learn about the nature

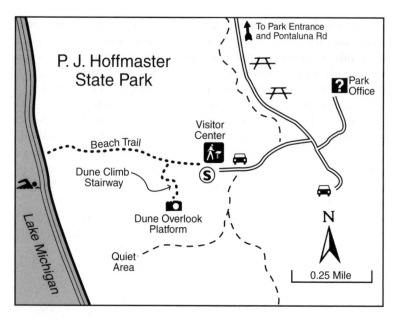

of dunes, and finish with a climb up to the Dune Overlook for an impressive view of them. Older families can undertake one of several trails that lead from the center through the interior of the park to the beautiful beaches along Lake Michigan. The trail offering the best views and the most direct route to the beach is Dune Climb Stairway.

The 1043-acre state park is reached by heading south of Muskegon on US-31 and exiting at Pontaluna Road, where you drive west for 3 miles to the park's entrance. Signs direct you toward the south end of the park road where the interpretive center is located. Gillette Visitor Center is open daily during the summer from 10:00 A.M. to 4:30 P.M. The schedule varies during the school year, so call for the current hours.

Built in 1976 to serve as Michigan's sand dune interpretive area, Gillette Visitor Center was extensively renovated in 2001. The two-story building is in fact overshadowed by a huge, windblown dune that is best viewed from a glass wall on the west side. On one side of the lobby is an eighty-two-seat theater where a multi-image slide show introduces visitors to the world of dunes and succession. On the other side is the center's exhibit hall, which uses interactive displays and computerized graphics to trace the origins of the Great Lakes sand dunes.

Gillette Visitor Center is an interesting place, but a lesson in sand dunes can only be complete with a view of them. Pick up the Dune Climb Stairway trail from the south side of the building, and you'll soon reach the stairway itself.

The wooden staircase is a climb of 165 steps up a steep dune. That's no easy stroll, but benches are positioned along the way for those hikers, young and old, who need to catch a breath. It ends at a viewing platform on top of the dune, 190 feet above the lake, where there is a display that identifies the surrounding land formations.

From the observation deck you'll see not only a panorama of Lake Michigan and its shoreline stretching before you, but dunes almost everywhere you look. Well forested or windblown, these steep hills of sand make up the majority of Hoffmaster's interior. Most visitors know they are viewing a portion of the world's most extensive set of freshwater dunes but don't realize these are among the youngest formations in Michigan, formed only 3000 years ago and constantly changing in their appearance, size, and effect on the environment.

From the platform, descend the steps (much easier than climbing them!) and continue west along the trail toward the beach. At one point the trail becomes a boardwalk with a interpretive plaque that explains the plant life of a dune environment. From there the trail breaks out of the cool shade of the hardwood forest to the desert-like setting of an open dune. Steps will help you descend to the beautiful beach along Lake Michigan, 0.5 mile from the visitor center.

Stay awhile to enjoy the surf and sun of Michigan's Gold Coast before returning to the visitor center.

40 SILVER LAKE SAND DUNES

Location ■ Silver Lake State Park
County ■ Oceana
Type ■ Day hike
Difficulty ■ Moderate to challenging
Hikable ■ April to November
Length ■ 3.6 miles, round trip
Fee ■ Vehicle entry fee
Information ■ Silver Lake State Park headquarters, 231-873-3083

For the boy or girl whose sandbox never has enough sand, there's the Silver Lake Sand Dunes, the mile-wide strip that separates the inland lake from Lake Michigan. This is heaven on earth for people who like to wiggle their toes in sand, climb steep slopes of sand, or run

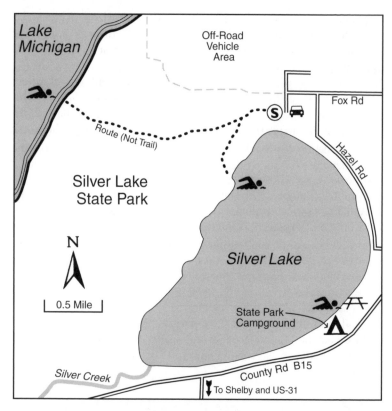

down dunes into a cool, refreshing lake. This, Silver Lake State Park rangers will say, is Michigan's own version of the Sahara Desert.

The 2936-acre state park is south of Ludington and reached from US-31 by exiting at Shelby Road and heading west 6 miles to County Road B15 (16th Avenue). Head north for 5 miles, past the state park campground entrance, turn west (left) onto Hazel Road, and follow the "ORV Access Area" signs. This will lead you to the dune pedestrian parking area.

The Silver Lake Sand Dunes are divided into three areas: Off-road vehicle (ORV) users enjoy their motor sport in the north; a dune ride concession operates in the south; and the middle is designated for hikers, who enter the area from a trail posted "Dune Access Stairway."

The short trail leads you through an oak and maple forest to a wooden stairway. On the top step you're face-to-face with a 50-foot-high wall of sand that is literally pouring into the forest. This dune is quite a climb, especially for young children, but once on top you're rewarded with a view of Lake Michigan on the horizon, Silver Lake to the left, and towering ridges of sand right in front of you. It's a striking contrast to go from the shady and cool forest at the trailhead to the world of rippled sand and brilliant sunlight.

The hike out to Lake Michigan is a one-way walk of 1.8 miles, with several steep slopes to climb. Families with children under the age of six or seven might choose to walk to Silver Lake instead, by heading south (left) at the top of the steps along the edge of the trees. It's a 10- to 15-minute hike to where the steep dunes form the north shore of the lake.

To reach Lake Michigan, select one of the ridges and begin scaling it. By climbing the one to the right (north), you will be able to watch the ORV daredevils racing along in a variety of vehicles: trucks with over-sized tires, four-wheelers, VW "Bugs," and homemade dune buggies. But the dune ridge straight ahead is visibly higher than those around it, and its sandy peak rewards you with the best vista in the park, including views of both Lake Michigan and Silver Lake.

Here the sand is pure and sugar-like, and there's not a plant around, not even dune grass. After trudging along the crest of the dune, you descend to the section where grass has taken root. Technically this is a trailless area, but several routes are visible through the grass and lead into the strip of oak and spruce pine. You can either put your trust into

In the Silver Lake Sand Dunes, with Silver Lake in the background

one of the routes or strike out on your own by just heading west.

It's about a 0.5-mile walk through the forest and then another short climb through windblown and grass-covered dunes before you reach the edge of a sandy bluff overlooking the Lake Michigan beach. What a beach! It is at least 30 yards wide and all sand, with the exception of an occasional piece of driftwood. The sand is smooth and almost white, the water is light blue, and there's often not another soul around.

41 SKYLINE TRAIL

Location ▪	Ludington State Park
County ▪	Mason
Type ▪	Interpretive walk
Difficulty ▪	Easy
Hikable ▪	April to December
Length ▪	1 mile
Fee ▪	Vehicle entry fee
Information ▪	Ludington State Park headquarters, 231-843-8671

Ludington State Park, at 5300 acres the largest state park along Lake Michigan, features more than 18 miles of trails. But the most popular path in the park is also the shortest: the Skyline Trail. Making this 1-mile loop requires you to climb stairways to the crest of a dune, but once you're on top the walking is easy and the views are spectacular.

The Skyline Trail begins and ends near the Great Lakes Visitor Center, one of eight state park interpretive centers. The center focuses on the creation and the importance of the Great Lakes that surround Michigan through a series of displays, hands-on exhibits, and a multimedia show. During the summer the center is open daily from 10:00 A.M. to 5:00 P.M. In May and September it is open only Friday through Sunday from 10:00 A.M. to 5:00 P.M., and is closed the rest of the year.

Ludington State Park is 8.5 miles north of the city of Ludington at the end of M-116. After passing the contact station but just before crossing the Big Sable River, turn east to reach the parking lot for the Great Lakes Visitor Center.

Three stairways provide access to the Skyline Trail. They are located in the parking lot for the visitor center, near the center itself, and along Sable River Trail. By following Sable River Trail and the Skyline Trail in a clockwise direction from the parking lot, you'll make a 1-mile loop and encounter the interpretive posts in numerical order.

You begin with Sable River Trail, which follows the south bank of the Big Sable River for 0.5 mile. You pass a footbridge across the river and then reach the Skyline Trail stairway closest to the Hamlin Dam. From a child's point of view the stairway looks like an endless series of steps to the sky. But the climb is a small price to pay for what awaits them at the crest of the dune. Once on top they'll discover the trail is really one long boardwalk.

Erosion of the sand dune prompted the park staff to replace the original trail with the wooden path in 1981. It was an immense project that took two years and included the Air National Guard using its helicopters to airlift much of the lumber to the top of the dune.

Though the trail on top is less than 0.5 mile long, there are numerous benches where you can sit and admire the stunning scenery. There are also thirteen numbered posts that correspond to an interpretive brochure available throughout the park. The topics range from identifying the three common evergreens in Michigan,

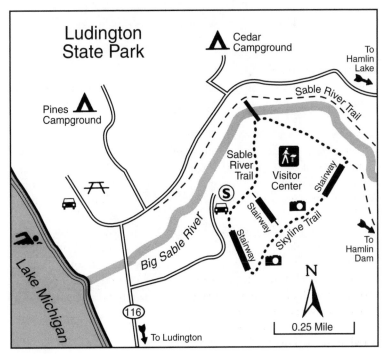

A stairway to the Skyline Trail in Ludington State Park

to dune-country succession, to the remnants nineteenth-century loggers left behind.

At post number 6 there are rows of benches where you can sit and view the Big Sable River emptying into Lake Michigan. An even more impressive panorama awaits you at post number 11. Here you can gaze south and see miles of open dunes stretched out to the Lake Michigan shoreline, the Ludington Harbor Lighthouse, and on a clear day even the Silver Lake Sand Dunes 25 miles away (see Hike 40).

After post number 13, you reach the third stairway that descends to the visitor center parking lot and completes the loop.

42 # NORDHOUSE DUNES

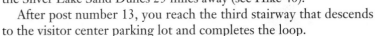

Location ■	Lake Michigan Recreation Area
County ■	Manistee
Type ■	Day hike
Difficulty ■	Moderate
Hikable ■	April to November
Length ■	2.4 miles
Fee ■	Vehicle pass or camping fee
Information ■	Manistee District Ranger, 231-723-2211

To reach the Lake Michigan Recreation Area in Manistee National Forest, once off US-31 you drive mile after mile after mile of woods and wetlands, with much wildlife (especially deer) but few signs of civilization other than the cars you pass. Arriving at the campground, children feel they are in the middle of the wilderness—and they are.

The recreation area lies at the northern end of Nordhouse Dunes, the only federally designated wilderness in the Lower Peninsula. It's an environmentally unique area that includes 4 miles of undeveloped Lake Michigan shoreline, 700 acres of open sand dunes, and 3450 acres of wooded dunes. Upon arrival, kids jump out of the car and are overwhelmed by what they see: mounds and even mountains of sand, miles of open beach, and the inviting waters of Lake Michigan.

This is paradise to them.

The recreation area features 100 rustic and wooded campsites well spaced along four loops. There are hand pumps for water, fire rings,

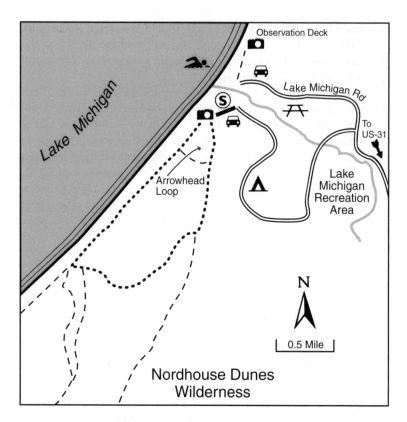

and picnic tables, but no electricity or showers. There is much to do for families during the day: swimming, beachcombing, scrambling up the stairs of two observation platforms. But hiking is the best way to see the area.

When Nordhouse Dunes was designated a wilderness area in 1987, the U.S. Forest Service removed the names of the trails, with the exception of the Arrowhead Trail. The campground is at the north end of Nordhouse Dunes' 10-mile network of trails where hikers can choose loops as short as 0.8 mile to an all-day hike of 6 miles. One of the best for children is a 2.4-mile hike that begins with the Arrowhead Trail and includes the first half of what used to be called the Michigan Trail.

Lake Michigan Recreation Area is reached from Manistee by heading south on US-31 for 10 miles and then right on Lake Michigan Road. The campground is at the end of the road, 8 miles from US-31. If you are not camping at the recreation area, a daily, weekly, or annual Huron-Manistee Recreation vehicle pass is required to park at the day-use area. In Manistee you can purchase a pass at the Manistee Ranger Station at 412 Red Apple Road, or at Northwind Sports at 400 Parkdale Avenue.

The hike begins with a scramble up the 122 steps of the southern observation platform, and if young hikers (or even Mom and Dad) can survive that, they shouldn't have too many problems with the rest of the route. The view was probably stunning at one time, but now it is partially blocked by treetops. Right behind the platform is a red trail post and map sign indicating Arrowhead Trail.

You can head either (left) inland or (right) toward Lake Michigan, but for most it's hard to pass up hiking along the shoreline first, one of the most scenic walks in the state. The trail actually follows a dune ridge high above the shoreline and is surprisingly level and easy walking. On one side are wooded hills, old dunes really, forested in hardwood, pine, and an occasional paper birch. On the other side is a steep drop, a strip of white sandy beach, and the blue horizon of Lake Michigan.

Within 0.3 mile of the platform you come to the junction of the Arrowhead Trail, the only cut-off point along the way. Head east (left) along the trail if anybody is having problems, and you'll be back at the platform in 0.5 mile. The entire Arrowhead Loop is generally considered a 30-minute walk, even with young children. Continue south,

Setting up camp at Lake Michigan Recreation Area in Manistee National Forest

however, for more of this enchanting walk along Lake Michigan, and in 0.8 mile you pass through a scenic stand of paper birch and then arrive at the junction of what use to be labeled the Middle Trail.

By continuing south along the lakeshore you will reach the open dunes but will end up hiking more than 6 miles by the end of the day. Head left (northeast) at the well-marked junction, and you leave the lakeshore and head inland along the Middle Trail. Sure, you're leaving the lake and beach behind, but tell the younger members of the group that this is where you might spot a deer or even a couple of them, especially halfway along the spur when it passes a wetland area. Listen for crunching leaves and look for that white flag that always signals a sudden retreat of deer.

The Middle Trail is a 0.7-mile walk inland and ends at a junction with the route formerly labeled Nipissing Trail. Head north, and in 0.3 mile you'll pass a gray water tower that looks totally out of place. Take a break—you're now only 0.25 mile from the campsite. Continue north, and the trail returns to the observation deck after passing two stairways, with the first leading down to the campground's Oak Loop and the second to Hemlock Loop.

Opposite: *Enjoying the sun and sand of South Manitou Island*

NORTHWEST MICHIGAN

43 PLATTE PLAINS TRAIL

Location ■ Sleeping Bear Dunes National Lakeshore
County ■ Benzie
Type ■ Overnight
Difficulty ■ Easy to challenging
Hikable ■ May to November
Length ■ Various loops of 3 to 7 miles
Fee ■ Vehicle entry fee
Information ■ Sleeping Bear Dunes National Lakeshore
park headquarters, 231-326-5134

Calling the Platte Plains area of Sleeping Bear Dunes National Lakeshore "plains" might be a little misleading. An aerial view of Platte Bay would clearly show the ancient shoreline sand dunes, which mark the successive positions of Lake Michigan after each intrusion of glacial ice melted. And from an airplane, the dunes might appear as gentle ridges. From the trails, however, they're steep hills. And to a child, they're mountains to be climbed.

Not to worry. The beauty of the Platte Plains Trail, a 15-mile network of various loops, is that you have your choice of how to hike into White Pine Backcountry Campground.

The longest loop is 7 miles, beginning from Platte River Campground, or you can choose a 5.6-mile loop that departs from a trailhead at the south end of Otter Lake. Both include a 0.8-mile stretch of steep, wooded dunes.

But if the children are young and new to the world of backpacking, Platte Plains can also be the destination for an easy and memorable experience of spending a night in Michigan's sand dune country. Part of the trail network follows old railroad grades, and from Peterson Road it's a one-way walk of 1.5 miles into the isolated backcountry campground. Even children under the age of six can tackle this 2-day adventure, since you backtrack to return to the car.

Begin the trip in Empire at the National Park Service headquarters on the corner of M-72 and M-22. Open from 9:00 A.M. to 6:00 P.M. daily, the visitor center has natural displays on the Sleeping Bear Dunes as well as information on other trails and activities and a three-dimensional map where kids and parents alike can see what they are

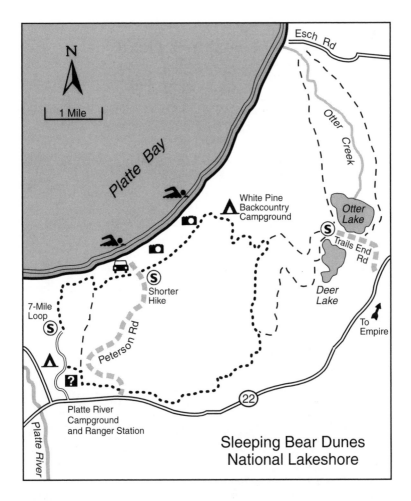

Sleeping Bear Dunes
National Lakeshore

about to climb (You're kidding!). Pick up a trail map to Platte Plains, or, if you want more detail, purchase the proper topographical quad.

From park headquarters, head south on M-22. Within 5 miles you reach Trails End Road, a dirt road that winds for a little over 1 mile around the south end of Otter Lake to a trailhead. This is the beginning of a 3.6-mile loop, and leads west (right) to a locator map at the junction with the spur to the backcountry campground. The walk-in facility is another 0.8 mile away through a rugged area of steep hills—forested dunes, actually.

Continue another 3.5 miles along M-22, and you'll reach Platte River Campground. Rebuilt in 1992 at the cost of almost $4 million,

Platte River is now one of the nicest campgrounds in the Lower Peninsula. The National Park Service facility offers 174 sites that include modern, rustic, and twenty-five secluded walk-in sites. There is also a ranger station where backcountry permits can be picked up. Near the walk-in sites at the north end of the campground is a trailhead for the start of the 7-mile loop, which includes the rugged dunes and 2.1 miles of hiking along the level bed of an old railroad grade.

But the shortest route to White Pine begins at the end of Peterson Road, a dirt road located just north of Platte River Campground, opposite Deadstream Road. Peterson winds 3 miles through the woods and ends at a parking area next to a beautiful stretch of beach along Platte Bay. Hike 0.25 mile back up the road and look on either side for the posts with green directional triangles near the tops. The trail to the west (right, with your back to Lake Michigan) returns to Platte River Campground, a walk of 1.3 miles. To the east is the trail to the backcountry facility; it begins in a semi-open area along a sandy path.

Within 0.4 mile you move into a thicker forest of oak and pine, but the trail remains level, right to the posted junction of a scenic lookout to Lake Michigan, a mile from Peterson Road. The lookout is a scramble out of the woods and into the windblown dunes, where you can view the entire bay, as well as the famous Sleeping Bear

Young backpackers take a break during a hike to White Pine Backcountry Campground.

Dunes to the north and South Manitou Island in Lake Michigan. The trail leaves the junction and follows gently rolling terrain that won't exert young children too much. Within 0.5 mile you reach the posted campground.

White Pine is located in a narrow ravine with wooded ridges running along both sides of the secluded sites. There's a vault toilet and a community fire ring, but no water, so backpackers must carry in whatever they expect to use. With only six sites, this area is a quiet section of the park, even during the busiest weekends when other campgrounds are overflowing. There is no view of the lake, but from site number 6 a short path wanders west through the woods and opens into an area of windblown dunes. From the high perch of the dunes you are rewarded with an expansive view of the park's famous features, Sleeping Bear Dunes and South Manitou Island (see Hike 48), while children will find the steep slopes of sand a tempting run.

Don't worry if they get sand in their hair during their mad dash down the dunes. Lake Michigan, with its clear waters and sandy bottom, is just a dune or two away. Return in the evening to sit on the last dune before the beach to watch the sun melt into Lake Michigan.

 EMPIRE BLUFF TRAIL

Location ■	Sleeping Bear Dunes National Lakeshore
County ■	Leelanau
Type ■	Interpretive walk
Difficulty ■	Moderate
Hikable ■	May to December
Length ■	2 miles, round trip
Fee ■	Vehicle entry fee
Information ■	Sleeping Bear Dunes National Lakeshore park headquarters, 231-326-5134

Empire Bluff Trail extends only a mile to the edge of a lakeshore dune, but few trails in Michigan and none in the Sleeping Bear Dunes National Lakeshore lead to a more spectacular view. The trail ends at the steep-sided edge of Empire Bluffs, which rise more than 400 feet above the sandy shoreline of Lake Michigan. Add six interpretive posts and an accompanying brochure that explains the natural and geological history of the area, and you have one of the best hikes in the state for children.

Due to the amount of climbing involved, this hike is a moderately challenging walk, but not nearly as hard as the Dune Climb (see Hike 46). Most families can hike out to the bluff, enjoy the view for a while, and return in under an hour. With older children, you can arrive before dusk on a clear evening to witness a sunset second to none. Just make sure you have a flashlight for the return hike to the car.

You can purchase a vehicle entry pass and obtain a map at the National Park Service visitor center on the corner of M-22 and M-72 in Empire. From the center, head south on M-22 for 1.7 miles and then west (right) on Wilco Road. The trailhead is to the left, a mile down Wilco Road.

The trail begins with a climb through the open fields of an old farm mentioned at post number 2, then moves into the cool shade of a beech-maple climax forest. In May these woods will be full of common trillium in full bloom. The walk levels out briefly when it skirts an old orchard, then resumes climbing across the hilly terrain of the perched dunes. The dunes are forested, so you are teased

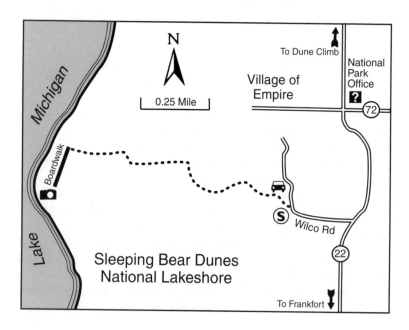

with only a brief glimpse between the trees of the magnificent view that lies ahead.

Eventually you descend to post number 5 and then make the final climb to post number 6, where you break out of the forest to a breathtaking panorama—a just reward for any young hiker who was lagging behind. You are more than 400 feet above the lake and can view Platte Bay to the south and Sleeping Bear Bluffs to the north, with the famous Sleeping Bear Dune itself appearing as a small hill on top of the high, sandy ridge. Seven miles out on the horizon is South Manitou Island. At this point, the trail swings south and follows a boardwalk along the bluffs for 500 feet to an observation platform with a bench. You could rest here for hours if so inclined.

45 COTTONWOOD TRAIL

Location ■ Sleeping Bear Dunes National Lakeshore
County ■ Leelanau
Type ■ Interpretive walk
Difficulty ■ Easy
Hikable ■ May to November
Length ■ 1.5 miles
Fee ■ Vehicle entry fee
Information ■ Sleeping Bear Dunes National Lakeshore park headquarters, 231-326-5134

Cottonwood Trail is an easy 1.5-mile loop in the open dunes of Sleeping Bear Dunes National Lakeshore. There are nine interpretive posts that correspond to a brochure explaining everything from blowouts to why dune sand is round. But the best thing about this trail is that it begins along Pierce Stocking Scenic Drive.

This scenic road is not long, a mere 7.4-mile loop, but mile-for-mile it offers more panoramic vistas than most other roads in Michigan. Named after the man who built it, Pierce Stocking Drive is a one-way loop with an interpretive brochure of its own and a speed limit of only 15 mph. There are so many scenic viewing points and pullovers that at times even 15 mph seems too fast.

The drive and the hike can be combined for an interesting afternoon that children as young as four or five can enjoy. Pack a lunch.

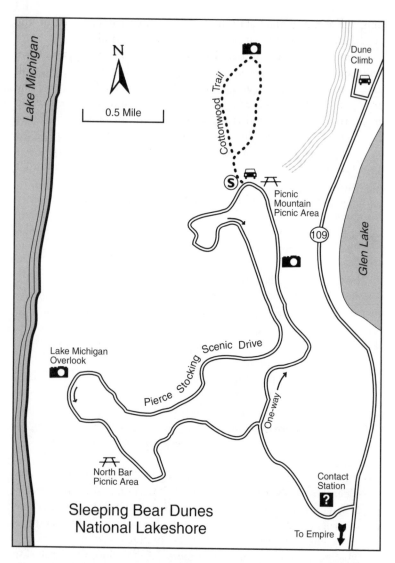

Sleeping Bear Dunes
National Lakeshore

There are two picnic areas along Pierce Stocking Drive, located before and after Cottonwood Trail. Both of them provide dining with a view.

Pierce Stocking Drive is 3 miles north of the National Park Service visitor center in Empire and is reached by heading northeast on M-22 and then turning north (left) onto M-109. The road is open for vehicles from May through mid-November from 9:00 A.M. until sunset. From a contact station at the entrance you can pick up the interpretive brochures for both the road and the trail.

There are twelve numbered stops along Pierce Stocking Drive, and the start of Cottonwood Trail is post number 4 where you will find a small parking area and a trailhead with a box of brochures. The first numbered post of the Cottonwood loop is right at the beginning of the trail, and for good reason: it warns you of poison ivy. From there you pass a huge blowout, a bowl-like dune carved by the prevailing southwesterly winds, and within 0.25 mile come to a junction. Head right to continue following the posts in numerical order counterclockwise.

Among the things you'll learn along the trail is that dune country is not a desert (it receives 30 inches of rain a year), that grains of sand reflect the colors of different minerals (quartz is the most common), and that beachgrass is one of the first stabilizing plants to grow on newly formed dunes.

The trail remains fairly easy until you past post number 6. Don't be alarmed; this is dune country, after all. In front of you will be a knee-bending climb to the halfway point of the hike. The climb is worth it, because at the top is a pair of benches and a great view. Spread out before you will be a spectacular landscape of the dunes, Glen Lake,

One of the many features of Pierce Stocking Drive in Sleeping Bear Dunes National Lakeshore is a covered bridge.

and the rolling countryside to the east. You can even see the Dune Climb (see Hike 46), where families and children will likely be charging down the famous slope of sand.

From the viewpoint you begin a steady descent that bottoms out in a stand of cottonwood trees. From here you're less than 0.5 mile from the parking lot, passing posts number 8 and 9 along the way.

46 DUNES TRAIL

Location ▪	Sleeping Bear Dunes National Lakeshore
County ▪	Leelanau
Type ▪	Day hike
Difficulty ▪	Easy to challenging
Hikable ▪	May to November
Length ▪	4 miles, round trip
Fee ▪	Vehicle entry fee
Information ▪	Sleeping Bear Dunes National Lakeshore park headquarters, 231-326-5134

Sleeping Bear Dunes National Lakeshore is a diverse landscape that includes birch-lined streams, dense beech and maple forests, and rugged bluffs that rise 460 feet above Lake Michigan. But the national park is best known for a 4-square-mile area of perched dunes on Sleeping Bear Plateau, and its famous Dune Climb, a 130-foot-high sand hill. Departing from the top of the hill is the Dunes Trail, the

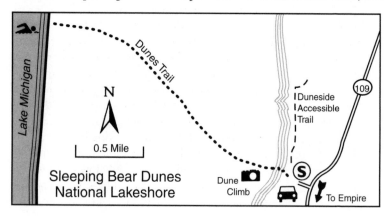

The run down the Dune Climb

shortest and quickest route to the Lake Michigan shoreline.

The Dune Climb is fun for children of any age. Those under the age of four usually run out of energy halfway up the steep slope of sand and are either carried the rest of the way by a willing parent or begin the run downhill from there. Older members of the family can easily make it to the top of the dune in about 15 minutes, where they are rewarded with excellent views of Glen Lake to the east, Lake Michigan to the west, and Sleeping Bear Point to the north. The trail out to the Great Lake, however, is considerably more challenging. The round-trip hike takes three to four hours on foot and should be attempted only by children seven years or older who are in shape and have some previous day-hiking experience.

Begin the day at the National Park Service visitor center, a nautical-looking building in Empire at the corner of M-22 and M-72, 22 miles west of Traverse City. The center is open 9:00 A.M. to 6:00 P.M. daily and features history and nature exhibits, a slide program, and a wall full of handouts about the park, including one on the Dunes Trail. From the visitor center head north on M-22, veer left onto M-109, and in about 6 miles you reach the Dune Climb.

The steep slope is only a few yards from the parking lot, store, and restrooms. Most visitors take off their shoes for the uphill climb in the warm sand and stop often to admire the view below or to watch others struggling up the dune. The top is marked by small stands of trees and a few benches that offer a shady place to sit and rest. The run down is exhilarating, to say the least, and often accomplished in a few minutes.

For those continuing on to Lake Michigan, remember that there is no water along the route and that the average hiker needs 30 to 40 minutes to cover a mile along the dunes. Fill a water bottle at the parking lot and pack along sunglasses, a hat, and sunscreen. Hiking boots or tennis shoes are necessary, as nobody should attempt this trail in bare feet.

The route begins by climbing the Dune Climb. Once on top, hikers strike out across the open rolling dunes, following blue-tipped brown posts that mark the 1.5-mile route to Lake Michigan. There are some stretches of gravel to cross, but for the most part this is an up-and-down hike across windswept dunes, which gently descend to Lake Michigan and a beautiful beach free of the crowds found elsewhere on the west side of the state. With children, plan on one and a half to two hours to reach the beach, and then follow the same route back to the Dune Climb parking lot.

47 SLEEPING BEAR POINT

Location ■	Sleeping Bear Dunes National Lakeshore
County ■	Leelanau
Type ■	Day hike
Difficulty ■	Moderate
Hikable ■	April to December
Length ■	4 miles, round trip
Fee ■	Vehicle entry fee; camping fees
Information ■	Sleeping Bear Dunes National Lakeshore park headquarters, 231-326-5134

Even when it's too cold to dip your toes into Lake Michigan or build a sand castle, the beaches of Sleeping Bear Dunes National Lakeshore can still be an intriguing place to take a child. That's because the park's shoreline is a trail of shipwrecks. The beaches are an excellent place to search for signs and pieces of century-old wrecks, because Manitou Passage was such a precarious channel to sail through. More than fifty ships have sunk in the narrow, deep passage between the Manitou Islands and the mainland, the vast majority of shipwrecks having occurred between 1850 and 1900.

Most of the ships ran aground close to shore, often within 400 yards of the beach. That makes the wrecks susceptible to storms, waves, and shoreline ice. Sometimes a hard blow will uncover a huge section of a hull. But more times than not, the forces of nature break off small pieces of the wreck and toss them ashore for hikers and visitors to puzzle over.

One of the best stretches to search is the 2 miles of shoreline from D. H. Day Campground west to Sleeping Bear Point. This makes for an easy and scenic beach hike of 4 miles, round trip. If that's too much for your troops, begin at the park's Coast Guard Station Maritime Museum, which is a 2-mile round-trip walk to Sleeping Bear Point.

At the Sleeping Bear Dunes visitor center, on the corner of M-72 and M-22 in Empire, purchase a vehicle pass and ask for the brochure entitled "Beachcombing for Shipwrecks." From the visitor center head north on M-22 and veer left on M-109. Within 5 miles you'll pass the Dune Climb and then curve right toward the town of Glen Arbor. You'll reach the entrance for D. H. Day Campground before entering Glen Arbor.

D. H. Day is an excellent facility with secluded sites, nightly ranger programs in July and August, and access to one of the finest beaches in a state known for great beaches. Although not directly on Lake Michigan, the National Park Service facility has eighty-eight sites

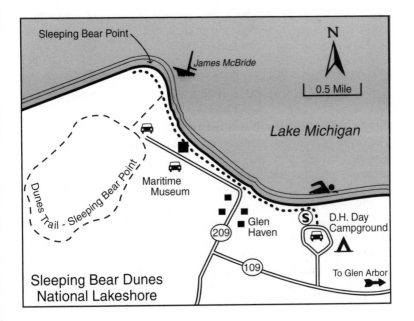

spread out in a rolling terrain of pines and hardwoods, none more than a five-minute walk from the water. All this plus its central location in the middle of the national lakeshore makes D. H. Day a very busy campground in the summer despite its lack of hook-ups for trailers, showers, or modern restrooms. The campground is filled nightly from mid-June through Labor Day. If you plan to camp at that time of year, either show up in the morning to claim a just-vacated site or keep heading north to someplace else.

Access to Lake Michigan from the campground is located near site number 55. The sandy path enters the trees but quickly emerges onto a shoreline where the sand is as fine as sugar, the water is turquoise in color, and the views are stunning. To the west you can see Sleeping Bear Dune, to the northeast Pyramid Point, and due north the Manitou Islands. If the day is clear you can even see the lighthouse on South Manitou Island.

Head west along the beach and keep one eye out for pieces of wrecks in the sand. Timber from ships is often white oak—black when wet, whitish when dry—with rounded edges or corners. Look for iron rings, spikes, pegs, or other fastenings attached to the wood—all telltale signs that the piece is from a wreck.

Within a mile you'll reach the Sleeping Bear Point Coast Guard Station Maritime Museum. The station was built by the U.S. Life-Saving Service in 1901 to assist the growing number of wrecks in Manitou Passage. It was originally located at Sleeping Bear Point, but when a dune threatened to engulf the buildings in 1931, the station was moved east into Sleeping Bear Bay. Today that lifesaving station has been restored as a maritime museum and, if it's open, is an appropriate rest stop in the middle of this shipwreck hike. The museum is open 10:00 A.M. to 5:00 P.M. daily from June to Labor Day and on weekends into early October.

From the station the beach swings northwest, and within 0.5 mile you pass a blue-tipped post that marks a junction. This trail provides access to the Sleeping Bear Point Loop, a 2.8-mile route that winds through open dunes and past ghost forests (standing trees killed by migrating sand). The loop is one way to add mileage to this adventure.

This hike stays on the beach, and in another 0.5 mile (2 miles from the campground) you'll reach Sleeping Bear Point. Be particularly alert along this stretch, as it's here you have the best chance of finding pieces of a wreck. Most of them being washed up are from the *James McBride*, a two-masted brig that went down intact in 1857. Timber and ironwork from the ship have been appearing on the beach since 1988. At

Hiking the Lake Michigan shoreline to Sleeping Bear Point

this point most families turn around and retrace their steps to either D. H. Day Campground or the maritime museum.

48 SOUTH MANITOU ISLAND

Location	■	Sleeping Bear Dunes National Lakeshore
County	■	Leelanau
Type	■	Day hike or overnight
Difficulty	■	Easy to moderate
Hikable	■	May to November
Length	■	6 miles, round trip
Fee	■	Ferry transport fee; vehicle entry fee; parking fee
Information	■	Sleeping Bear Dunes National Lakeshore park headquarters, 231-326-5134; Manitou Island Transit, 231-256-9061

Combining a scenic boat ride, the charm of Leland's Fishtown, and beautiful beaches, South Manitou Island is one of the best hiking adventures for children in Michigan. The 8-square-mile island is part of the Sleeping Bear Dunes National Lakeshore and has a fascinating natural and human history, including a restored lighthouse, its own set of sand dunes, and even a shipwreck that can be viewed from shore. The island was the site of a farming community and a lifesaving station in the mid-1800s, but today the dirt roads are footpaths and the only

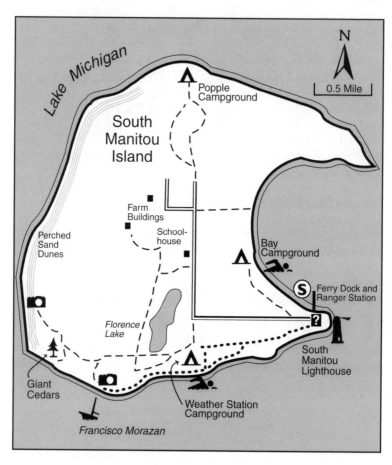

vehicles allowed on South Manitou are those of the National Park Service rangers and a concessionaire who offers a tour of the island.

This hike to the wreck of the *Francisco Morazan* can be either a day hike or turned into an overnight backpacking adventure by spending the night at one of the island's three campgrounds. If you plan it as a day hike, keep in mind that the ferry schedule allows you and your troops only five hours to cover a round-trip walk of 6 miles. If you stay overnight, you'll need to pack in all necessary equipment, food, and supplies. There are no stores or restaurants on South Manitou Island.

The port of departure for South Manitou Island is Leland, a small town in the heart of the Leelanau Peninsula on M-22. The fun begins before you even set foot on the island. You depart from Leland's quaint Fishtown, an old commercial fisherman's wharf whose docks and weather-beaten buildings have been restored, giving this outing a sense of "high seas" adventure for kids. From the end of the wharf a Manitou Island Transit passenger ferry departs for the island at 10:00 A.M., sailing daily June through August, and on Friday through Monday plus Wednesday in May, September, and October. The boat arrives at the island at 11:30 A.M., where it docks until its departure at 4:30 P.M. The 1.5-hour boat ride is scenic, and children find it an exciting way to begin a trip. Reservations are accepted and are recommended for weekends in July and August. Parking is available near the ferry office for a small fee.

When you arrive at the National Park Service dock and ranger station, pick up a trail map. If you plan to stay overnight, obtain a free backcountry permit and register for a site at one of three campgrounds: Popple, Bay, and Weather Station. This hike passes through Weather Station Campground, which is the best choice for children, as the 1.4-mile, one-way walk from the ferry dock to the campground can be handled even by hikers as young as four or five. The trail is well posted and begins between the visitor center and the South Manitou Lighthouse. It's a walk in the woods, with most families stopping only to search for the thimbleberries that ripen in late July and August. The trail finally breaks out along the high banks above Lake Michigan where the campground is located. There are some excellent campsites here, overlooking a sandy beach below and Sleeping Bear Dunes off in the distance on the other side of Manitou Passage. There is good swimming anywhere on the island.

To reach the battered wreck of the *Francisco Morazan*, carefully descend the bluff from the campground to the beach below. It's

A family admires the shipwreck off South Manitou Island in Sleeping Bear Dunes National Lakeshore.

roughly 1.5 miles along the shoreline from the campground to the southwest corner of the island, where you can view the freighter 200 yards offshore. It's an easy walk unless a tree has tumbled down the bluff and is lying across the beach; in that case you'll have to bypass it by wading in the water. The *Francisco Morazan* ran aground in 1960 when its captain mistakenly thought he was rounding Beaver Island 100 miles away. Today almost half of the ship, midsection to stern, sits above the lake's surface.

The easiest way to return is to remain on the beach all the way back to the ferry dock. It's a 3-mile walk on the beach, and for much of the last 1.5 miles you'll be able to see the top of the South Manitou Island Lighthouse. If you're overnighting on the island, don't pass up the excellent lighthouse program that ends with visitors climbing the spiral staircase for an impressive view from the top of the tower.

49 SAND LAKES QUIET AREA

Location ▪	Pere Marquette State Forest
County ▪	Kalkaska/Grand Traverse
Type ▪	Day hike or overnight
Difficulty ▪	Easy to moderate
Hikable ▪	May to November
Length ▪	Loops of 2.5 to 7.2 miles
Fee ▪	None
Information ▪	Kalkaska office, Department of Natural Resources, 231-258-2711

My father remembers the Sand Lakes. In the 1930s, his uncle and aunt would pile him into an old Ford, along with a picnic lunch of cold fried chicken, and head south from their summer place in Elk Rapids, past Williamsburg to where the road ended. Here they followed old logging trails that were little more than two sandy ruts to the group of five small lakes. They would fish, swim, or just enjoy their meal in the quiet setting that the area offered.

Little has changed since then. The red pines are taller, you now have to hike in instead of drive, and a thick undergrowth of ferns has turned some of the logging roads into footpaths. But parents still arrive with their children to show them what a world without vehicles,

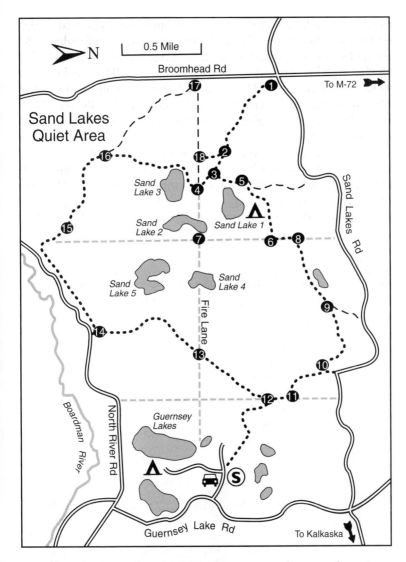

motors, and man-made noise is like. You come to listen to the quiet.

Designated in 1973 by Michigan's Department of Natural Resources, the Sand Lakes Quiet Area is a 2500-acre preserve of rolling forested hills, interspersed with twelve lakes and ponds and connected to one another by a 12-mile network of trails and old logging roads. The trails form a 7.2-mile loop beginning at Guernsey Lake State Forest Campground. With a backcountry campground located almost halfway around the loop on the edge of Sand Lake number 1, it makes for an excellent backpacking opportunity for children six to eight years old. The trails are wide, well marked with locator maps, and, for the most part, easy to follow.

Even children younger than six can enjoy an overnight trip by beginning at a trailhead at the corner of Sand Lakes Road and Broomhead Road, 4 miles south of M-72 after departing on Cook Road. From there the hike from post number 1 to 2, 3, and finally 5, the site of the walk-in campsite, is a one-way trek of 1.2 miles.

Guernsey Lake can be reached from Kalkaska by heading west from M-72 on Island Lake Road for 8 miles and then turning south on Guernsey Lake Road to the posted state forest campground. The rustic facility has thirty-six sites, including many that overlook the lake from a high bank, and a boat launch. These campsites are available on a first-come, first-served basis.

Just before entering the campground, you pass a parking area on the entrance drive, with a trailhead and map box across from it. This trail is a forested spur to post number 12 on the main loop. Along the way you pass the northern arm of Guernsey Lake (appears as a pond on some maps) and in 0.7 mile come to the junction.

The shortest route from the junction at post number 12 to the

One of many lakeside views along the Chain O' Lakes, Pere Marquette State Forest

backcountry campsite is the 2-mile northern half of the loop (right); while the trail leading south (left), a wide path through a forest of pines, oaks, and maple, reaches Sand Lake number 1 in 3.7 miles. Heading south, you soon come to a fire lane that veers off to the left and then Pit Lake, a small, round body of water, not on many maps.

From Pit Lake the trail heads straight for post number 13 and then continues south to post number 14. Along the way you pass unmarked trails to Sand Lake number 5, which might be a little confusing, but the main loop will be marked with blue blazes on the trees. At post number 14 you swing west and parallel the North River Road scenic drive from above (though you rarely see the road), then descend to it at a well-posted junction. Continue north on the trail, and you'll soon reach post number 15.

The trail returns to an old logging road and eventually descends to an open area of tall shrubs and saplings. This is a good place to look for deer, especially near dusk. If you can't find the animals themselves, search the sandy path and you're sure to spot their tracks crisscrossing in every direction. At post number 16 the main loop swings north and continues following the logging road for 0.2 mile; but at one point the old road ascends a ridge forested on top and the loop, poorly marked here, veers off to the left.

You pass a boggy area, reenter the woods, and then emerge at Sand Lake number 3, a clear body of water where occasionally an angler will hike in to fish for bass. The trail skirts the lake and then arrives at post number 4. With the backcountry campground only a short walk away, just beyond post number 5, the first day is almost over. The facility is on the edge of Sand Lake number 1 and has a pair of vault toilets, a table, and a water pump near the lake. It's a shady, and very quiet, area with enough space for a half dozen tents.

It's a 0.5-mile walk to post number 6. From there the trail ascends to post number 8 and then swings east toward post number 9. Along the way the trail passes another small, unnamed lake where on a still evening you can watch the panfish rise and snatch bugs off the surface. Mushrooms in an assortment of colors grow in profusion along this stretch. The trail to post number 10 becomes a footpath through the woods as it weaves its way through the gently rolling terrain. This is perhaps the most enjoyable stretch of the loop, but it ends all too soon as you arrive at a locator map and return to following the wide logging road. At this point you are only a mile away from your vehicle, via post numbers 11 and 12, and the spur to the state forest campground.

50 SKEGEMOG SWAMP PATHWAY

Location ■ Skegemog Lake Wildlife Area
County ■ Kalkaska
Type ■ Day hike
Difficulty ■ Easy
Hikable ■ April to November
Length ■ 2 miles, round trip
Fee ■ None
Information ■ Kalkaska office, Department of Natural Resources, 231-258-2711

What did we expect? Hike in a swamp in the middle of the summer, and there's going to be something trying to land on us. In this case, deerflies in Skegemog Swamp. My family was hustling down the trail, each of us waving one hand above our head in an attempt to keep these voracious flies from landing, when suddenly we all put on the brakes.

Whoa! Red dots along the trail, thousands of them, which could only mean one thing. Raspberry heaven! We were the fastest one-armed pickers you ever did see.

Besides being a wildberry paradise, Skegemog Swamp is also one of the most scenic wetlands in Michigan with one of the driest trails to it. The area is protected as the Skegemog Lake Wildlife Area, a preserve of 1300 acres that was saved from developers by the Michigan Chapter of The Nature Conservancy working with the Department of Natural Resources.

There are several viewing points of this sensitive area, including Skegemog Overlook, a roadside park on M-72 8 miles west of Kalkaska, where you can enjoy lunch while viewing the lake. But for the best view of the wetlands that border the lake, hike the Skegemog Swamp Pathway, an easy 1-mile walk out to an observation tower.

Approach Skegemog Lake Wildlife Area from M-72 by taking County Road 597 toward Rapid City. Within 4 miles you will see the posted trailhead and parking area for Skegemog Swamp Pathway. The pathway is an interesting adventure anytime of the year, but bring bug repellent in the summer, and binoculars during the spring and fall, to watch the migrating waterfowl.

Observation tower and boardwalk at the end of the trail through Skegemog Swamp

The pathway passes through three distinct habitats. From the parking lot, you enter a predominantly beech forest, carpeted in ferns, and then arrive at a former railroad grade. A lone trail marker directs you south along the old railroad bed for 0.5 mile to a bridge leading into the woods. It's along the open, meadow-like terrain of the rail-trail where the raspberries can be thicker than the deerflies.

The final habitat is the lush woods of a cedar swamp. Here the trees were primarily cedar, spruce, and tamarack, which grow well in the bog-like conditions and shade a forest floor carpeted in moss, wintergreen, and wildflowers earlier in the summer. Jack-in-the-pulpit, with its white flower in the green pulpit, is one of the easiest flowers for children to recognize. There are also Canada mayflower, grass of Parnassus with its flower of five white petals, and great blue lobelia with its delicate bluish-purple flowers.

The trail follows a stream through the woods and consists of a boardwalk with scattered benches much of the way. Toward the end you cross the stream on a bridge and shortly emerge into the open area of cattails and marsh grasses, with the observation tower at the end of the boardwalk, 0.5 mile from the railroad grade. The tower is 16 feet high and provides a sweeping panorama of Skegemog Swamp, a maze of open-water channels and patches of cattails and other shrubs. On the horizon is the edge of the lake, and with the aid of binoculars you can often spot a variety of bird life, including Canada geese, great blue herons, a variety of waterfowl, and, if you're lucky, a bald eagle or osprey.

51

SEDGE MEADOW TRAIL

Location ■	Grass River Natural Area
County ■	Antrim County
Type ■	Interpretive walk
Difficulty ■	Easy
Hikable ■	April to November
Length ■	0.7 mile
Fee ■	Donations
Information ■	Grass River Interpretive Center, 231-533-8576

Kids like boardwalks. Wooden trails keep their socks dry, their boots clean, and them out of the doghouse when they inadvertently wear their tennis shoes on a muddy outing. But most of all, where there is a boardwalk there is usually a swamp, marsh, or bog surrounding it.

That's the best part—exploring these environments that are packed with interesting plants and wildlife without being knee-deep in black ooze. At the Grass River Natural Area there is an abundance of boardwalks—in fact, some trails are nothing but boardwalks, because a good slice of this 1037-acre park is either a sedge meadow, marsh, or cedar swamp.

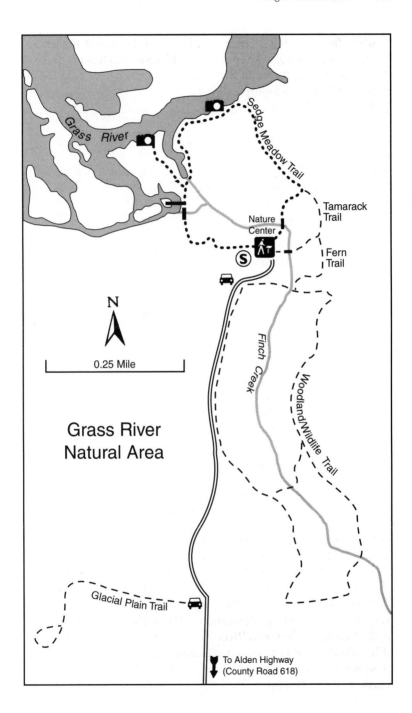

Grass River

Sedge Meadow Trail

Nature Center

Tamarack Trail

Fern Trail

(S)

N

0.25 Mile

Grass River
Natural Area

Finch Creek

Woodland/Wildlife Trail

Glacial Plain Trail

To Alden Highway
(County Road 618)

The Grass River itself is only 2.5 miles long and just chest deep. It's a crystal-clear waterway that connects Lake Bellaire to Clam Lake as part of Antrim County's Chain of Lakes. But the extensive floating sedge mats and other wetlands that surround the river are so intriguing that they prompted a fund-raising effort to purchase the land and dedicate it as a natural area in 1976. They've been building boardwalks ever since.

The natural area has six trails that total 5 miles and are marked with interpretive posts. Woodland/Wildfire Trail is longest at 2.2 miles, while the 0.25-mile-long Tamarack Trail is designed to be handicapped accessible. But our favorite is Sedge Meadow Trail. This 0.7-mile loop is one long boardwalk through the most intriguing habitat in the park.

From US-131 in Mancelona, Grass River Natural Area is reached by heading west on M-88 toward Bellaire. When M-88 swings sharply to the north in 2 miles, continue west on Alden Highway (County Road 618). The entrance road to Grass River is posted along CR-618 before you reach Alden. The park is open from dawn to dusk year round, and the interpretive center is open daily 10:00 A.M. to 4:00 P.M. June through August.

Begin at the small interpretive center. Inside there are several rooms of displays and a small bookstore where you can purchase a copy of the trail guide that corresponds to the markers on all the trails.

Sedge Meadow Trail begins behind the interpretive center and is followed in a clockwise direction. You begin in the forest but quickly enter wetland habitat where plants have been identified and numbered posts correspond with the trail guide. At times you can view showy lady's slippers and other orchids, floating sedge mats, Labrador tea, bog cranberry, and, my son's favorite, the bug-eating pitcher plants.

In less than 0.25 mile the trail emerges at the edge of Grass River where an observation tower has been built on the boardwalk along with a series of benches. Just beyond it a spur leads to another elevated viewing platform on the river, and at post number 13 a third observation area. All three decks will aid you in spotting not plants but wildlife, as almost fifty species of mammals alone have been identified within the natural area. Dawn and dusk are the best times to be here, quietly standing on the tower scanning Grass River, Finch Creek, and the edge of Clam Lake. Wildlife sighted from the tower includes river otters, mink, white-tailed deer, and a variety of bird life including marsh hawks, ospreys, and bald eagles.

From post number 13 the trail begins looping back toward the interpretive center. Within a few hundred yards you reach a junction with Tamarack Trail and then cross Finch Creek for the second time. The visitor center is just on the other side.

5**2** DEADMANS HILL

Location ▪ Mackinaw State Forest
County ▪ Antrim
Type ▪ Day hike
Difficulty ▪ Moderate
Hikable ▪ May to November
Length ▪ 3 miles
Fee ▪ None
Information ▪ Gaylord office, Department of Natural Resources, 989-732-3541

Begin this hike with the story about Stanley Graczyk. The twenty-one-year-old was a fun-loving lumberjack in the early 1900s, known as "Big Sam" to his friends and fellow loggers. On May 20, 1910, Big Sam was to marry his childhood sweetheart. That day, Sam's crew was working the steep ridges of the Jordan River Valley, with Big Sam himself driving a team of horses and a "Big Wheel" loaded with timber down the ridge. Poor Stanley never even made it to the altar. The huge cart slipped out of control and ran over him, killing

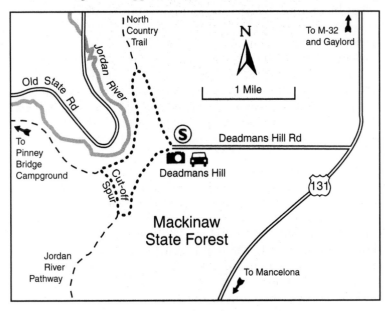

him instantly. It's been called Deadmans Hill ever since.

Today it's a scenic spot with views of much of the Jordan River watershed, and an especially popular destination during the height of fall colors. But the top of Deadmans Hill also serves as the trailhead for the Jordan River Pathway, a 2-day backpacking trip of 18.7 miles, and Deadmans Hill Loop, a 3-mile day hike that combines a walk in the woods with a little bit of logging lore. The short loop includes a downhill section in the beginning and some uphill walking at the end, but the trail is wide, easy to follow, and a hike that can be accomplished in a pair of sturdy tennis shoes.

The walk begins and ends on top of Deadmans Hill, located off US-131, 11.5 miles north of Mancelona or 6 miles from the hamlet of Alba. From US-131 turn west onto Deadmans Hill Road and follow it for 2 miles. The end of Deadmans Hill Road is a loop and includes a small parking area and the trailhead for the Jordan River Pathway, marked by a large trail sign and a box to leave your hiking plans. Before arriving, fill up your water bottles. There are vault toilets at the overlook but no drinking water.

From the spectacular views on top of the ridge, you begin the trip by dropping quickly into the valley. The long descent to the valley floor lasts 0.6 mile, but along the way you pass several tree identification signs. The first is a rare one in Michigan, pointing out an elm tree that somehow survived the spread of Dutch elm disease in the 1960s. You bottom out at a junction where the North Country Trail merges with the Jordan River Pathway, and then take a sharp 180-degree swing to the south.

For the next 0.5 mile the trail skirts Deadmans Hill, with the bluff rising steeply above and below you, and a mile from the trailhead you arrive at a gate. Parts of the Jordan River Pathway were re-routed in the mid-1990s, and the gate is used to block the old route. The trail now descends to an observation deck where you can watch a spring pump cold, clear water in the Jordan River. The gurgling is almost nonstop for the next 0.3 mile as you cross several more feeder creeks beneath the cool shade of giant cedars.

At 1.3 miles you break out to views of Deadmans Ridge, and in another 0.2 mile you arrive at a junction where backpackers continue west but you swing south. The cut-off spur first moves through an open area where sandy soil supports a healthy crop of wild berries. If it's early to mid-summer, have the children search low to the ground for strawberries. If it's high summer, then it's raspberries you're after, and in mid- to late August blackberries will appear. This portion of

Enjoying the view from Deadman's Hill

the trail might take you a while to get through. It's hard for a young hiker to pass up a ripe berry.

Eventually the trail reenters a young forest and begins a steady climb. Just when young legs are ready to give out, you top off at a posted junction. The trail from the west is the return of the backpacker's route, while the one to the east is the path to the parking area. The walk is an easy 1.1 miles from here to the end, with only a slight climb now or then.

53   AUSABLE RIVER TRAIL

Location ■	Hartwick Pines State Park
County ■	Crawford
Type ■	Interpretive walk
Difficulty ■	Moderate
Hikable ■	April to November
Length ■	3 miles
Fee ■	Vehicle entry fee
Information ■	Hartwick Pines State Park headquarters, 989-348-7068

The best-known foot trail in Hartwick Pines State Park is the Pines Loop, a mile-long paved path that begins at the Michigan Forest Visitor Center and includes virgin white pines and a reconstructed logging camp. The interpretive center and the trail provide a fascinating look at lumberjacks and shouldn't be missed on any visit to

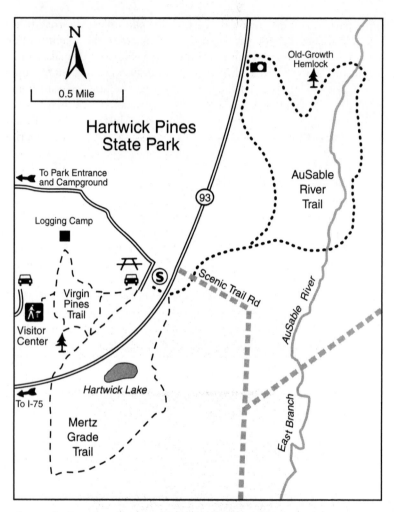

the park. But for a quieter, less crowded, and certainly more intimate look at nature, lead your children along AuSable River Trail on the east side of M-93.

The 3-mile trail features two crossings of the East Branch of the AuSable River, stands of virgin timber, and sixteen interpretive posts that correspond to descriptions in a brochure available at the park headquarters or the interpretive center. A little bit of climbing is involved and a few wet spots must be crossed, but overall the trail is not difficult and provides a 2-hour escape from the often busy portion of the park.

Hartwick Pines is 9 miles north of Grayling and reached from I-75 by departing at exit 259. Head north on M-93 for 2 miles, and at the park's main entrance turn east (right) and follow the road to the picnic area at the end, passing up the entrances to the Michigan Forest Visitor Center and campground. The visitor center makes an interesting stop before the hike. During the summer the center is open 8:00 A.M. to 7:00 P.M. daily. After Labor Day the hours are shortened to 9:00 A.M. to 4:00 P.M., and the center is closed on Monday.

From the picnic area parking lot, both Mertz Grade Trail and AuSable River Trail begin together by crossing M-93 to the clearing where the park's old campground was once located. The two split here, with AuSable River Trail crossing the dirt road called Scenic Trail that borders the clearing.

AuSable River Trail leads you through a stand of pines to reach the junction with the return loop; bear right, and you'll cross an old vehicle track in 0.4 mile. In another 0.25 mile you reach the East Branch for the first time, where interpretive post numbers 5 and 6 are clustered. There is a bench here, and if you sit quietly long enough you might see the rings of rising trout forming and then dissolving in the stream's current. Post number 6 marks an old swimming hole, built during the 1930s by the CCC (Civilian Conservation Corp) as a place for them to cool off after long days of planting pine saplings. Trout fingerlings can often be seen darting around its still waters.

The trail moves through a mixed forest of white, red, and jack pine intermixed with maple, balsam, and paper birch, and at 1.3 miles you reach the second bridge over the East Branch. The trail might get a little wet on the other side, and post number 10 explains the reason: you're in a cedar swamp. The best stand of trees, however, is an area of virgin hemlock at 1.7 miles. The huge pines tower above the trail, making most children pause to study their

Footbridge over the East Branch of the AuSable River along the AuSable River Trail

grandeur and the shafts of light filtering down between them.

The relatively level walk turns into a climb when you begin walking up a glacial moraine to reach post number 13 at 1240 feet. There was once a scenic overlook here, but the view has been significantly reduced by a growth of saplings. A glimpse of the ridgeline 4 miles away is still possible, especially if some members of your hiking party sit on your shoulders. After a descent from the ridge, the final leg of the trail is a level walk past a railroad grade of the Lewiston Railroad and a rectangular mound that many believe was once a barn.

54   AVALANCHE PEAK

Location ▪	Avalanche Peak Park
County ▪	Charlevoix
Type ▪	Day hike
Difficulty ▪	Challenging
Hikable ▪	May to November
Length ▪	0.5 mile, round trip
Fee ▪	Donation
Information ▪	Boyne City Chamber of Commerce, 231-582-6222

I don't think there's ever been an avalanche at Boyne City's Avalanche Peak, but the hill is incredibly steep—so steep that in the 1950s, it was a downhill ski area with tow ropes and even a chairlift. Today the hill is a city park and best known in the winter as a place to go for some daredevil sledding.

During the rest of the year, the hill is a wonderful peak for children to climb. A stairway assists them with the long ascent, and from the top they can enjoy some of the most panoramic views in the Lower Peninsula. Pack a lunch along, and you can spend an hour or more at the top.

 From US-131, take M-75 into Boyne City. Once in town, head west on Division Street and then turn left on Lake Street. The entrance to Avalanche Peak Park is posted at the south end of Lake Street.

Near the parking lot is a warming lodge with restrooms, used mainly in the winter by ice skaters, cross-country skiers, and sledders. Towering above the lodge is Avalanche Peak. Thank goodness there is a stairway to the top!

Cut across the base of the hill to that endless stairway, and begin climbing. It's 473 steps to the top (we know, we counted them!), but a

series of benches allows you to pause and catch your breath.

The peak is a grassy knoll where the city has thoughtfully built an observation deck with several benches. There isn't a better view below the Mackinac Bridge than what greets you from the top of Avalanche Peak. At your feet is Boyne City, while stretching out to the west is Lake Charlevoix dotted with sailboats. Surrounding the lake are ridges and hills that in October are painted in burnt-orange shades of Halloween.

Talk the kids out of running down the hill, and use the stairway to descend back to the parking lot.

At the top of Avalanche Peak

55 BALSAM AND CEDAR TRAILS

Location ■	Thorne Swift Nature Preserve
County ■	Emmet
Type ■	Interpretive walk
Difficulty ■	Easy
Hikable ■	May to November
Length ■	1 mile
Fee ■	Vehicle parking fee
Information ■	Thorne Swift Nature Preserve office, 231-526-6401

A mere 30 acres in size, Thorne Swift Nature Preserve is not big and contains only a mile of footpaths. But compacted within this small area is a variety of habitats and—if you're a child—a lot to do. Thorne Swift protects a special slice of the Lake Michigan shoreline just off M-119, the scenic drive known as the "Tunnel of Trees." Within the preserve is a cedar swamp and pond followed by a strip of small coastal dunes and finally the lakeshore beach, all linked by three short interpretive trails.

You can spend an hour or two here hiking the trails and enjoying the nature center. Or, pack along bathing suits, beach towels, and a swimmer's mask and snorkel, and you can spend the afternoon searching for Petoskey stones or looking at fish in the shallow waters of Lake Michigan.

To reach Thorne Swift Nature Preserve from Harbor Springs, head north on M-119 for 4 miles and then follow Lower Shore Drive as it descends to Little Traverse Bay. The preserve is reached within 0.5 mile on Lower Shore Drive. The nature center is open only during the summer from 10:00 A.M. to 7:00 P.M. daily. There is a small parking fee at the preserve, or you can walk or ride a bicycle in for free.

Begin at the Elizabeth Kennedy Nature Center where there are discovery boxes, a touch table, live species on display, and a Native American exhibit constructed by the Little Traverse Band of Odawa Indians.

The most important display for many, however, is on Petoskey stones. Michigan's state stone is petrified coral, leftover fragments of the many reefs that existed in the warm-water seas that stretched from Charlevoix to Alpena 300 million years ago during the Paleozoic Era. Dry Petoskey stones are silvery with no markings apparent to the untrained eye, but when the fossils are wet it's easy to see the honeycomb pattern that covers them. Gem enthusiasts love them, and you can see them polished and for sale in jewelry shops throughout northern Michigan. You can also search for them yourself later at the lake.

From the center three interpretive trails depart into the woods.

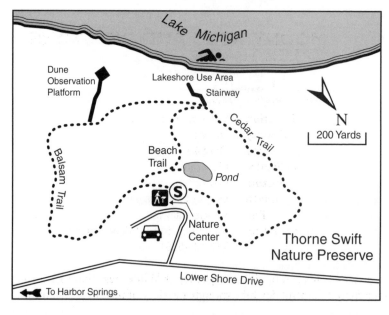

Heading south is Balsam Trail, which immediately enters a cedar swamp and within 0.25 mile arrives at a long boardwalk. This wooden trail extends from the trees to an observation platform perched above the open dunes. The sudden transition of moving from a cool, dark woods to the hot, dry dunes isn't lost on anybody, not even kids.

Among the displays at the observation deck is one devoted to tracks. Children can study pictures of prints on the plaque, and then look down and see them for real in the dunes: porcupine, white-tailed deer, red fox, ring-billed gulls. Naturalists have even reported seeing bear tracks occasionally.

From the boardwalk, Balsam Trail skirts the edge of the forest and quickly arrives at the junction with the Beach Trail and Cedar Trail. Also located here is a stairway that descends through the dunes to the preserve's Lakeshore Use Area, a pebbled beach where that recently acquired knowledge of Petoskey stones can be used. You can search the shoreline for the state stone or cool off with a swim in the crystal-clear waters of Little Traverse Bay. This is also a good area for snorkeling. Children can swim around the large boulders offshore and see a variety of marine life including fish.

The quickest return to the nature center is the Beach Trail, a walk of less than 0.25 mile that includes an interesting pond. Cedar Trail is a little longer (around 0.25 mile) but includes ten numbered posts that correspond to a brochure available at the nature center.

56 MOUNT NEBO AND BIG STONE CREEK TRAILS

Location ■ Wilderness State Park
County ■ Emmet
Type ■ Day hike
Difficulty ■ Moderate
Hikable ■ May to November
Length ■ Loops of 3.9 to 4.6 miles
Fee ■ Vehicle entry fee
Information ■ Wilderness State Park headquarters,
231-436-5381

Four short trails can be linked together at Wilderness State Park to make for a delightful day hike though a variety of terrain and natural features. The trek includes following a stream where there is a considerable amount of beaver activity, climbing to the top of Mount Nebo for a glimpse of Lake Michigan, and exploring the perimeter of several small ponds laden with wildlife.

Best of all, the main trailhead is located just a step away from the park's two campgrounds—one situated along the sandy shore of Big Stone Bay, and the other in a grove of mature pines. Combine a night in the campground with the day hike in the morning and an afternoon spent on the bay's beautiful beaches, and you've put together an enjoyable outdoor adventure for children of any age.

The east entrance for Wilderness State Park is 8 miles west of Mackinaw City and is reached by following County Road 81 and continuing west on Wilderness Park Drive after crossing Carp Lake River. On summer weekends through Labor Day, the campgrounds at Wilderness State Park are extremely busy and often filled. For advance campsite reservations, call the Michigan State Parks Central Reservation System (phone 800-447-2757).

Three of the four trails—Pondside, Red Pine, and Hemlock—have interpretive posts, and the corresponding brochures can be obtained at the park headquarters or the contact station. You can shorten the loop to 3.9 miles by heading left at the Pondside trailhead and beginning with Red Pine Trail.

The trailhead for Pondside Trail is located a short walk from the Pines Campground entrance and is marked by a large display map. Pondside Trail is a 0.7-mile loop around Goose Pond, with interpretive posts numbered clockwise, but many prefer hiking it in the opposite direction to avoid backtracking the top portion in continuing on to the 1.25-mile Red Pine Trail. The trail never leaves the edge of the pond and features fifteen posts pointing out a variety of trees and other plants. At the south end, it crosses three wooden bridges, two of which run along beaver dams, allowing you to view the animal's handiwork: sticks on one side, mud on the other.

Red Pine Trail departs east at post number 7 of Pondside Trail and immediately passes through a swamp area that at times can present a challenge to keeping your shoes dry. You climb out of the lowlands in 0.4 mile at post number 7 and follow a ridge to emerge at the trail's namesake halfway through the hike: a beautiful stand of red pine. You pass two small ponds, descending to the second, larger one after first viewing it from above. Frogs will be croaking here and turtles scrambling off logs for the security of the water. If the bugs are not too bad, it's hard not to pause in search of other critters. Be-

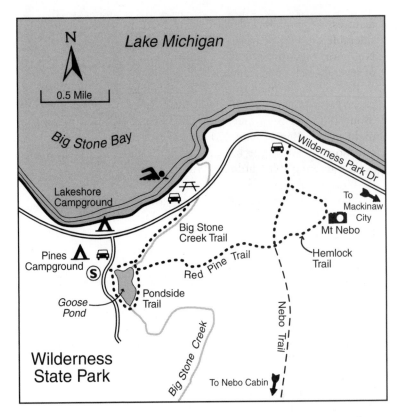

yond the second pond, the trail crosses one more swampy section to douse any shoes that have remained dry up to this point, and then ascends to a junction with Nebo Trail.

Beginning just a short way up Nebo Trail is the 0.7-mile Hemlock Trail, a climb to the top of Mount Nebo. The first half is a steady but gradual march up the hill until you reach post number 24, the high point where the stone foundation of an old fire tower remains. Not much of a view during the summer, but in the spring and fall you can see Lake Michigan to the north through the bare trees. The trail rapidly descends the peak and then passes some old-growth hemlock at post number 26, huge trees more than 200 years old.

From the north end of Hemlock Trail, it's 0.25 mile north along Nebo Trail to Wilderness Park Drive and then 0.9 mile along the county road to the posted trailhead of Big Stone Creek Trail, across the parking lot from the park's day-use area. The trail is a level 0.7-mile walk that soon comes to Big Stone Creek and then follows it to

Anglers fishing Goose Pond in Wilderness State Park

where man has dammed it to create Goose Pond. In the middle of the walk you'll see where beavers have dammed the creek themselves, causing it to flood the original trail. Today you can still see the side of the old trail in the middle of a pond. There are some great examples of gnawed trees surrounded by wood chips, and even a couple of beaver lodges, the best and largest 0.2 mile from the man-made dam. Eventually Big Stone Creek Trail merges into Pondside Trail, and it's only a short walk west to the trailhead and display map.

Opposite: *Hiking in the Horseshoe Bay Wilderness*

EASTERN UPPER
PENINSULA

57 HORSESHOE BAY WILDERNESS

Location ■	Hiawatha National Forest
County ■	Mackinac
Type ■	Day hike or overnight
Difficulty ■	Moderate
Hikable ■	May to November
Length ■	2.5 miles, round trip
Fee ■	None
Information ■	St. Ignace Ranger District, 906-643-7900

On the way to Horseshoe Bay Wilderness, you pass Castle Rock with its sprawling gift shop and larger-than-life statues of Paul Bunyan and Babe, the blue ox. Also Fort Algonquin, a stockade that looks like it belongs on the set of the television show "F-Troop." Then several motels, a party store, and finally a casino, whose parking lot on the weekends overflows with tour buses, hotel vans, and recreational vehicles.

This is wilderness???

One of the thirteen wilderness tracts created by the 1987 Michigan Wilderness Act, Horseshoe Bay is not the smallest such area at 3790 acres, but it's definitely the closest to an interstate. In some places I-75 is less than 100 yards from its western border, and on most summer weekends the traffic is so heavy, the trucks rumbling past so loud, it's almost impossible to escape the noise in this slice of the Hiawatha National Forest.

This is wilderness???

Label it what you want: wilderness, wild, or simply a quick escape from the maddening crowds and tourist traps surrounding the Mackinac Bridge area. One thing is for sure, Horseshoe Bay is unique. Located only 3 miles from the St. Ignace city limits, Horseshoe Bay has changed little since loggers passed through at the turn of the century. For the most part the tract is a series of low, forested ridges separated by narrow, shallow swamps, whose dense cedar stands are especially attractive to deer.

The outstanding feature of this wilderness, however, is 7 miles of undeveloped shoreline in Lake Huron's St. Martin Bay. Horseshoe Bay itself is a beautiful beach, where the sand is smooth and the water is a tropical turquoise in color. Best of all, the hike in is short, and if you carry in a tent you can spend the night.

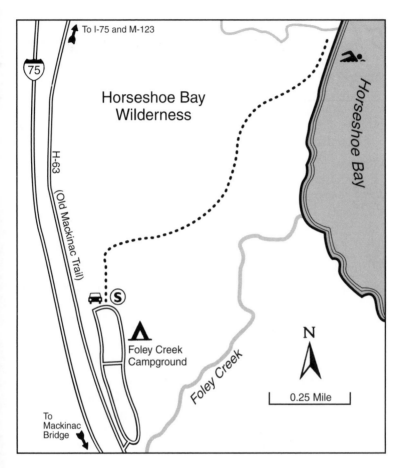

This is a wilderness made for kids.

The Horseshoe Bay trailhead is in Foley Creek National Forest Campground. To reach the U.S. Forest Service campground from I-75, depart at exit 348 and head east. Follow campground signs that will lead you north along H-63 (also known as Old Mackinac Trail) to the entrance of Foley Creek Campground.

From the back of the single loop of sites, the trail enters a birch and maple forest but within a half mile begins winding through the cedar swamps, crossing them on thick beams. If the day is dry, the hike can be slippery in spots and soggy if you step off the planking. If it is raining, then this is a slog through mud and standing water.

But the swamps are interesting, a cool and shaded world even on the hottest day where you can see pitcher plants and other insect-hungry vegetation. Within a mile you return to the drier maple forest and then at 1.2 miles from the campground break out of the trees to the sandy shoreline of Horseshoe Bay.

The southern end of the bay lies outside Hiawatha National Forest, and you can see the end of a road and a small cabin. But if you pitch your tent with the door angled to the north, all you see is sand and surf stretching toward Grosse Point and the pines that border the shoreline. The site is first come, first served; no permit is necessary to camp.

The only way to return to Foley Creek is to backtrack along the trail you followed in.

58 CUT RIVER NATURE TRAIL

Location ▪	Cut River Gorge Roadside Park
County ▪	Mackinac
Type ▪	Day hike
Difficulty ▪	Moderate
Hikable ▪	May to December
Length ▪	1.5 to 2 miles
Fee ▪	None
Information ▪	Michigan Department of Transportation Welcome Center in St. Ignace, 906-643-6979

Cut River Gorge Roadside Park is actually three parks clustered along US-2, a place where motorists can pull off and stretch their weary legs on that long drive across the Upper Peninsula. Connecting the roadside parks are two trails and an impressive bridge, making the gorge a destination for a short but scenic hike.

The trails and the bridge can be combined to form a 1.5- to 2-mile loop that descends to the river and a beautiful beach along Lake Michigan. Keep in mind that it's a climb of almost 150 feet to return to US-2, but there are plenty of benches along the way where young hikers can stop and catch their breath before pushing on.

 The roadside park is 26 miles west of St. Ignace or 16 miles east of Naubinway. Two parks straddle US-2 on the east side of the gorge, while the third is north of the road on the west side.

Begin at West Park where the West Trail is well posted. The trail immediately enters the woods surrounding the rest area and begins a

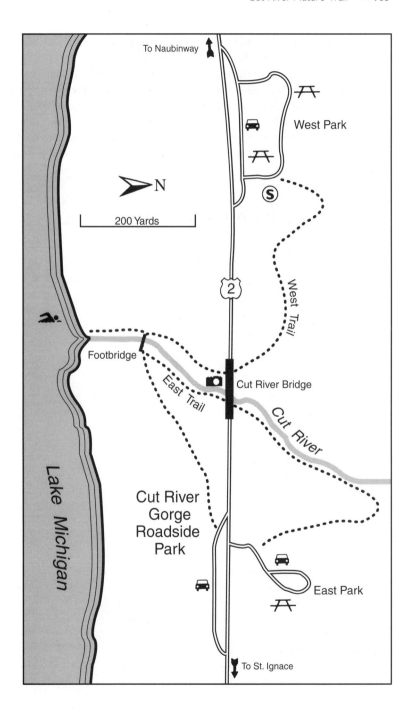

To Naubinway

West Park

N

200 Yards

2

West Trail

Footbridge

East Trail

Cut River Bridge

Cut River

Cut River
Gorge
Roadside
Park

Lake Michigan

East Park

To St. Ignace

S

steady descent toward Lake Michigan. Within 0.25 mile you pass underneath the Cut River Bridge. Built in 1948, the steel cantilever bridge is as an impressive sight from underneath as it is from on top. The bridge is 641 feet long, stands 147 feet above the river, and contains 888 tons of steel. If it's a busy travel day, you'll hear vehicles rumble across it above you.

Once beyond the bridge you spot the Cut River and then descend to where it leaves the gorge and flows into Lake Michigan. Stretching out in each direction here is the sandy shore of the lake, a great place to swim or build sand castles. Back inside the gorge, the gurgle of the river is louder than the hum of traffic on US-2, while a footbridge leads across the river to the East Trail. This trail begins by following the Cut River for almost 0.25 mile and then makes a steady climb out of the gorge to emerge at the back side of East Park.

You can return to West Park via a sidewalk along the highway bridge, pausing in the middle to peer down into the gorge or enjoy a sweeping view of Lake Michigan. This would be a 1.5-mile hike that takes most families less than an hour to walk. The alternative is to cross to the pull-off on the south side of US-2 where a stairway of 231 steps takes you back down to the footbridge across the Cut River. You would then backtrack the West Trail for a 2-mile loop.

59 BIG KNOB AND CROW LAKE TRAILS

Location ▪	Lake Superior State Forest
County ▪	Mackinac
Type ▪	Day hike
Difficulty ▪	Easy to moderate
Hikable ▪	May to November
Length ▪	0.5 mile and 2.5 miles
Fee ▪	None
Information ▪	Naubinway office, Department of Natural Resources, 906-477-6262

A "Big Knob" to climb, an assortment of trails to hike, and one of the most beautiful beaches along Lake Michigan. What more could a kid want in a campground? As for the parents, the best part of Big Knob recreation area in Lake Superior State Forest is the lack of crowds.

Maybe the facility fills up during the Fourth of July weekend, but the rest of the summer you can usually count on getting a site in the rustic campground. Arrive during the middle of the week or at the end of August to obtain a site just inside the towering pines along the Lake Michigan shoreline, where your tent will be only a few steps from the golden sand and light blue waters of Lake Michigan.

The area is reached after driving the scenic lakeside portion of US-2, beginning with a trip over the Mackinac Bridge. From I-75, head west on US-2 for 50 miles, passing through Naubinway and then turning left (south) on Big Knob Road. It's 6 miles along the narrow and winding road to the campground on Lake Michigan, and along the way you'll pass the trailheads for two of the three treks in the area. The third, Marsh Lakes Pathway, is a 1.5-mile trail that begins from the parking area of the campground's picnic area.

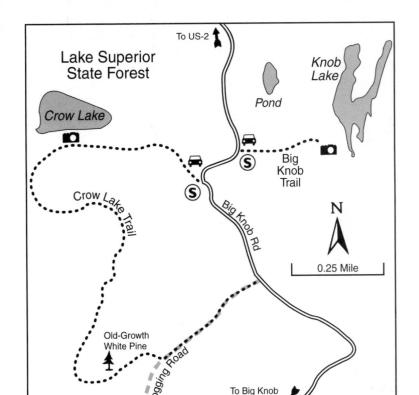

The shortest trail is the 0.25-mile climb to Big Knob, a high point on a forested sand dune. The posted trailhead is 2.5 miles north of the campground (3.5 miles south of US-2 along Big Knob Road), right across the parking area from Crow Lake Pathway. Big Knob Trail is basically a steady, but not overly exerting, climb to the viewing point, where there is a bench and a U.S. Geological Survey marker.

Along the way are three sets of log stairways and a view of a small pond to the north. The trail ends at the top of Big Knob where you are greeted with a panorama of Knob Lake below and the marshland that surrounds it. It's an excellent view, especially in spring and early fall when large flocks of Canada geese often use the lake as a stag-

Enjoying the Lake Michigan beach at Big Knob Campground

ing area. You see them and hear them, and often the honking greets you before you even begin the hike.

Crow Lake Trail has three trailheads, including the first right across from Big Knob. It's a 2.5-mile loop to walk the trail and return along Big Knob Road to your vehicle. From the first trailhead, you begin with a steady climb to the top of a sand dune ridge and then follow the gently rolling contour of its crest. Within 0.3 mile you come to the posted junction with the second trailhead and then at 0.7 mile a good view of Crow Lake.

After passing above the lake, the trail gently descends from the ridge and passes through open areas that feature an impressive growth of ferns. But if it's August, examine the ground along the trail (or have the children do it—they're closer to it, anyhow). This is blueberry country, and if the timing is right there will be dots of blue all over the place. At 1.3 miles, the trail passes the largest of several marsh areas.

You climb up and over a low dune ridge and then emerge at a

rather interesting area. To the right is a clear-cut, and to the left a preserved stand of old white pines, some so large two people couldn't connect their hands around them. All of this demonstrates the multiple-use concept of state forest management, which may mean little to most children. What will have a profound effect on them is the sign that reads "Lightning Damaged Pine." Behind it are a pair of white pines that are broken in half, the tops of their massive trunks shattered into a dozen pieces.

You reach an old logging road at 1.8 miles with a few more interpretive signs that make this an educational as well as a scenic hike, and at 2.1 miles you return to Big Knob Road. It's a 0.4 mile walk up the road to the first trailhead.

60 PINE RIDGE NATURE TRAIL

Location ▪ Seney National Wildlife Refuge
County ▪ Schoolcraft
Type ▪ Interpretive walk
Difficulty ▪ Easy
Hikable ▪ May to mid-October
Length ▪ 1.5 miles
Fee ▪ None
Information ▪ Seney National Wildlife Refuge headquarters, 906-586-9851

At Pine Ridge Nature Trail we saw nature almost as soon as we stepped out of the car. Located at Seney National Wildlife Refuge, the 1.5-mile interpretive trail begins at the visitor center, and we had no more parked the car than a handful of Canada geese strolled within three yards of us, one with five goslings trailing behind her.

"It's wearing a green necklace," my son said.

"It's an identification band," I replied.

That's how close we were, but that's why we had come—to get close to wildlife, especially the winged variety.

Established in 1935 after loggers and ill-informed farmers ran roughshod over the land, today Seney is a rich mosaic of forests, rivers, pools, and swamps—especially swamps—spanning 95,455 acres in the central Upper Peninsula. It is estimated more than two-thirds

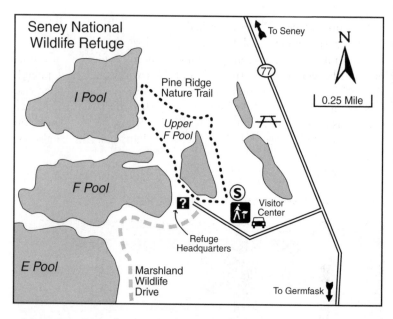

of the refuge is wetlands, which attract more than 200 species of birds to the area.

Canada geese you'll have no problem spotting, but the charm of Pine Ridge Nature Trail is the opportunity to see such grand species you rarely see back at home: loons, sandhill cranes, even a bald eagle soaring overhead.

Seney is reached from M-77 by turning west onto a posted refuge road 2 miles north of Germfask or 5 miles south from the town of Seney. Follow the refuge road to the visitor center.

Begin with the impressive visitor center, built on a large pond with one side a huge glass wall set up with telescopes so visitors can view the bird life on the surrounding marshes. There are also displays on the history, ecology, and wildlife of the refuge, hands-on exhibits for children, and an auditorium that shows nature films every hour. The interpretive center is open 9:00 A.M. to 5:00 P.M. daily from mid-May to October.

Pine Ridge Nature Trail begins just north of the visitor center and is followed counterclockwise. You quickly arrive at the first interpretive plaque along the loop. Since spotting wildlife is the theme of this trail, the plaque provides some helpful hints in doing just that: avoid sudden moves, try to blend into the surroundings, look for shapes and motions rather than the animal itself, and, most of all, "Become a Nature Detective."

"Nature detective?" my son asked.

"They want you to look for droppings," I replied.

The trail passes between two ponds (where "evidence" of musk-rats and beavers is easily spotted) and then winds around Upper F Pool. Within 0.3 mile you come to a bench on a small, shaded rise overlooking the water. If the bugs aren't too bad, if there is any breeze at all, this is how you watch wildlife on Pine Ridge Nature Trail: you sit down on the bench at dusk and see what happens. Almost always, something does.

Within 0.75 mile, the trail departs from Upper F Pool and begins

A family of Canada geese at Seney National Wildlife Refuge

following sections of boardwalk through swamps. This is the most interesting stretch. You hike through a swamp and then climb a small rise forested by red or jack pine, a "pine ridge" that provides an excellent vantage point to study the marsh you were just in.

The trail passes through another marsh and then climbs the second pine ridge. Within a mile you emerge at I Pool, which looks more like a lake than a diked-up body of water. In the middle of the pool are dozens of nesting islands where it's possible to spot more bird life. Eventually the trail swings southeast, passes within sight of the refuge headquarters overlooking F Pool, and then returns to the visitor center.

61 LOWER TAHQUAMENON FALLS

Location ■	Tahquamenon Falls State Park
County ■	Chippewa
Type ■	Day hike
Difficulty ■	Easy
Hikable ■	May to mid-October
Length ■	I mile
Fee ■	Vehicle entry fee; boat rental fee
Information ■	Tahquamenon Falls State Park headquarters, 906-492-3412

Our day in Tahquamenon Falls State Park began at the Upper Falls, the second or third largest waterfall east of the Mississippi River, depending on whether you're measuring water volume or length of drop. My children, cascade connoisseurs from almost the time they could walk, were deeply impressed with this Upper Peninsula jewel that measures 200 feet across, descends 50 feet into a sea of mist and foam, and has a thunder that can be heard from the minute you step out of the car.

We began the day here but we spent most of it 4 miles downriver, where we rented a rowboat from the park concession as the first step to viewing the Lower Falls. As far as children are concerned, the Upper Falls are impressive but the Lower Falls are much more fun.

While not nearly as stunning, this series of cascades are still beautiful and are best viewed by combining a boat trip across the river with a short walk around an island, an outing ideal for any short-legged hikers.

Tahquamenon Falls State Park is on M-123 between Paradise and Newberry and has separate day-use areas for the Upper and Lower Falls. The Lower Falls are 12 miles west of Paradise and 23 miles northeast of Newberry. The rowboats may be rented from May through mid-October (call park headquarters for details). At Lower Falls there are 176 modern campsites split between the two loops. Because of the popularity of the park, the sites can often be filled from

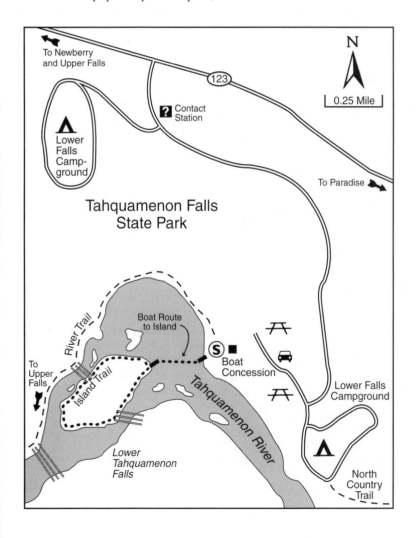

July through mid-August. Also passing through the campgrounds is the North Country Trail, the national trail that will span 3200 miles from North Dakota to New York when completed.

The boat trip across the Tahquamenon River is a short and easy row. From where you pick up the rowboat, you can see the long dock on the small island. Row to the dock and tie up your craft.

At the dock a stairway leads to the beginning of the trail. Step for step this is one of the most beautiful footpaths in the state, only there are not a lot of steps. This loop of less than a mile skirts the perimeter of the island, passing one display of tumbling water after another.

Head right, and you'll immediately come to the first series of descents where you'll learn why the Lower Falls are so popular. During the summer parents and children alike will be kicking off their shoes, wading out on the ledges of this drop, and letting the river cascade across their legs.

Try doing that at the Upper Falls.

From here the trail alternates between boardwalks and a well-manicured path that winds through shady cedars and other pines but always stays in view of the river. At the back of the island you can look upriver to see another set of falls, and a little farther on you arrive at the final and largest one of them all, a set of cascades that combine for a 22-foot drop over layers of shale.

Just before you return to the dock, the trail passes an observation platform on the island's northeast corner that provides a good view of the Tahquamenon River, finally free of falls and flowing toward the cold waters of Lake Superior. At the dock you can retrieve your rowboat for the trip back to the mainland.

Lower Falls in Tahquamenon Falls State Park

62 AUSABLE LIGHT STATION

Location ■	Pictured Rocks National Lakeshore
County ■	Alger
Type ■	Day hike
Difficulty ■	Easy
Hikable ■	May to November
Length ■	3 miles, round trip
Fee ■	None
Information ■	Grand Marais Ranger Station, 906-494-2669

Pictured Rocks National Lakeshore is a nice place to visit during the summer. It's spectacular during late September, when the fall colors are at their peak and the Indian summer sun brings out the colors of these sandstone formations towering over Lake Superior (such as Miner's Castle in Hike 63). But many feel the best time to undertake this adventure is in November, when the skies are gray and Lake Superior is crashing along the rocky shoreline. The camping might be a little chilly and it could even snow then, but there's not a better backdrop for enjoying the unusual maritime flavor of this trail.

This easy and level walk combines the rugged shoreline of the Great Lake with scattered remains of shipwrecks and the preserved AuSable Light Station. One, of course, is directly responsible for the other. The stretch from AuSable Point, where the lighthouse is perched, to Whitefish Point to the east was known as "the graveyard of the Great Lakes" to sailors in the 1800s, as dozens of ships perished along the exposed shoreline. The AuSable Light Station was built in 1874 and manned until the U.S. Coast Guard automated it in 1958. Today there is still a light at the top of the tower to warn ships of the shoals off AuSable Point, while the rest of the station is now listed on the National Register of Historic Places and under the care of the National Park Service.

Just getting to the trail is an adventure. Begin in Grand Marais with a stop at the Maritime Museum and ranger station. Open when staffing is available in July and August, the museum, a former lifesaving station, features uniforms, a Lyle gun, and other equipment used

by the lifesaving crew that lived there. From the small and picturesque town, head west on County Road H-58, past Grand Sable Lake
and the sand dunes trying to creep across the road. From here the
road plunges into a thick forest as it curves and winds its way toward
Munising, a 50-mile trip. Your stop is Hurricane River Campground,
12 miles from Grand Marais.

Head to the lower level of the campground, a pleasant area to pitch
a tent, where every site is a short walk from the sandy beach. The
shoreline makes for a nice stroll, but Lake Superior is usually too
cold for even the bravest (most foolhardy?) souls to swim in. A bridge
crosses the Hurricane River and allows the Lakeshore Trail, a 40-
mile route through the park from Grand Marais to Munising, to continue through the campground. It merges with an old lighthouse
access road on the east side, marked with a gate. Before you head
down the old track, though, the "Shipwreck" sign next to it will have
you and your kids scrambling down to the beach. These ruins lie
about 20 yards off the beach and are hard to see clearly when there is
a chop on the water. Tell the children not to be disappointed; better
ones lie ahead.

The old track follows the shoreline from above, and soon you see
the sandy beach give way to a rocky coast. Some stretches are strewn
with small boulders, while others are solid slabs of red rock whose

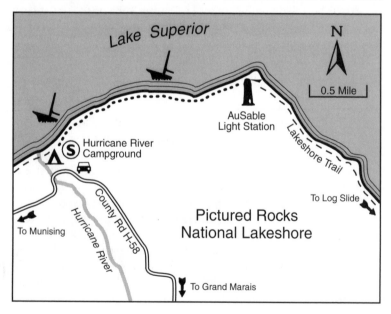

Inspecting shipwrecks along the Lakeshore Trail, Pictured Rocks National Lakeshore

surface has been sculpted into a series of ripples by centuries of waves washing ashore. At almost a mile from the gate you arrive at the second shipwreck sign. After descending to the beach, it's 1500 feet east (right) to the first remains, lying on the beach; the timbers, still joined by ironwork, are recognizable as the former hull of a ship. Two more sets of ruins lie farther up the beach. Return to the trail by backtracking to the sign.

The light station is only a short walk from the shipwrecks and features a number of buildings: keeper's residence, boathouse, fog signal house, even a red brick privy. But the most impressive structure by far is the lighthouse, with its tower projecting light 107 feet above Lake Superior. Interpretive displays throughout the station explain the history and functions behind each building. The lighthouse itself was renovated in the early 1990s and is open to the public as part of a ranger-led tour. The tours are held every half hour from noon to 5:00 P.M. daily July through Labor Day. The best part of the tour, maybe even the entire hike, is the climb to the top of the tower. It's 100 steps up to view the original Fresnel lens inside and the sweeping Grand Sable Dunes outside.

63 MINERS FALLS TRAIL

Location ■ Pictured Rocks National Lakeshore
County ■ Alger
Type ■ Interpretive walk
Difficulty ■ Moderate
Hikable ■ May to November
Length ■ 1.2 miles, round trip
Fee ■ None
Information ■ Pictured Rocks National Lakeshore headquarters, 906-387-2607

If the tour buses and crowds get to be too much for you at Miners Castle, the famed nine-story monolith at Pictured Rocks National Lakeshore, there is a quick and easy escape nearby. Just before ending at the large day-use area overlooking the rock formation, Miners Castle Road passes the trailhead to Miners Falls.

The Miners River begins to the south, near the town of Shingleton, and on its way to Lake Superior flows over its namesake falls and through Miners Lake. The area was first visited in 1771–72 by Englishman Alexander Henry, who arrived looking for "leaders," or indicators of mineral deposits. His party of geologists found one in the discolored water oozing from nearby bedrock and named the waterway the Miners River. It's one of those funny little twists of history, because the area never did yield any valuable minerals. But today the trail to the falls is priceless as a quick escape from the mobs swarming the overlook at Miners Castle.

Miners Falls Trail leads from the road to an observation deck overlooking the cascade, for a round trip of only 1.2 miles. Though short, it does include a stairway of seventy-seven steps, and that's just enough to keep most souvenir-laden tourists at bay. The trail is also an interpretive walk with eleven posts that correspond to a brochure available at the trailhead.

This walk can be accomplished by most kids, but if you have small children, do keep a close eye on them when using the stairway. Spray from the falls can make the wooded steps and platform slippery at times.

The Miners Falls trailhead is 9 miles from Munising. From the National Forest Information Center on M-28 on the east edge of town, take County Road H-58 east, bypassing the turn-off to Munising Falls.

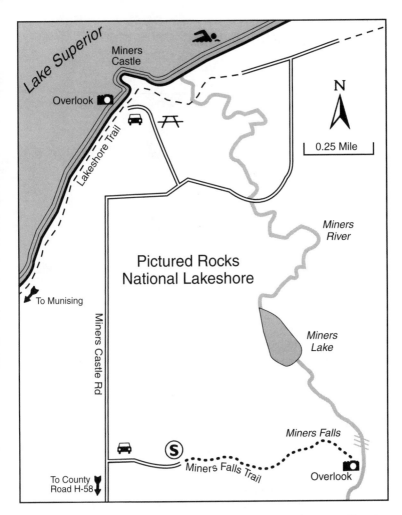

Turn left (north) onto Miners Castle Road, and in 5 miles you will arrive at the posted entrance to the small parking area for Miners Falls Trail.

From the small parking lot you enter a Northern mixed hardwood forest, dominated by American beech whose gray bark in the fall resembles elephant legs. At one point you skirt the edge of a ridge and in late fall, when enough leaves have fallen, can gaze down into a large basin below, the setting for Miners Lake and the pine forest that surrounds it.

Within a half mile the path turns into a stairway, a steep set of steps, often wet and a little slippery from the clouds of mist created by Miners Falls. But the descent is worth it. You end up at a small platform, overlooking the thundering volume of water that comes roaring over an inland section of the Pictured Rocks escarpment (described in the Introduction under "Michigan's Geography, Geology, and Weather"). The stage is a rocky gorge with the tea-colored river outlined by the lush green of spruce, fir, cedar, and other conifers that thrive around the cascade.

There are benches here, so bring a snack and take a break to enjoy the rainbow of hues reflected in the rising mist by the sun. Most likely the observation deck will be all yours until the next visitors, trying to escape the humanity at Miners Castle, appear descending the steps.

Hiker enjoying Miners Falls in Pictured Rocks National Lakeshore

You return to the parking lot by the same trail. There are benches built into the stairway for quick rests during the ascent back to the top of the ridge.

64 TYOGA HISTORIC PATHWAY

Location ▪	Escanaba State Forest
County ▪	Alger
Type ▪	Interpretive walk
Difficulty ▪	Easy
Hikable ▪	May to November
Length ▪	1.4 miles
Fee ▪	None
Information ▪	Marquette office, Department of Natural Resources, 906-228-6561

A lost logging town was rediscovered when the personal accounts of two Upper Peninsula men were pieced together with newspaper articles, county historical records, and labor records, allowing Tyoga to emerge from a faded past. Based on the information and photos that were found, the Tyoga Historical Pathway was built in 1988 and today provides families not only a pleasant forest walk but an interesting glimpse into a turn-of-the-century lumber town.

Spurred on by the nation's growing demand for white pine, a group of Pennsylvania businessmen purchased the eventual townsite of Tyoga and 1200 adjacent acres in 1902. When the Tyoga Lumber Company was incorporated in 1905, three million board feet of logs had already been cut from the woods surrounding the thriving lumbering town.

The 1.4-mile loop is an easy hike but wet at times, and boots are recommended most of the summer. Along the way there are twenty-two interpretive posts, each providing in words or photos a view of life in old Tyoga. Plan on 45 minutes to an hour to walk the trail and read the interpretive signs.

The logging pathway is located 23 miles west of Munising, via M-28. Turn north at the Deerton turn-off and follow Campground Road for 2 miles to a small parking area and the trailhead. At one time

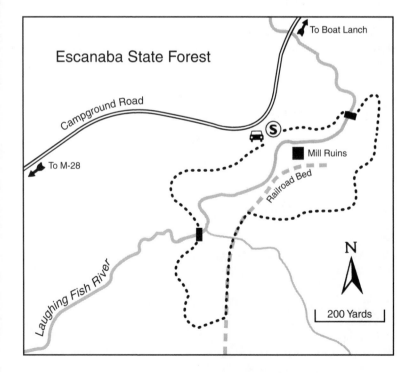

there was also a state forest campground here, but that was closed in the early 1990s.

The trail begins on the banks of Laughing Fish River (as it was known then), and the first few posts discuss the millpond that was formed and the two-story mill powered by an Atlas steam engine. You can still see the foundations that held the 130-horsepower engine whose bandsaw could cut 50,000 board feet of pine and hemlock in ten hours.

From here the trail crosses a bridge over the river, follows the opposite banks briefly, and then swings into the woods. Along the way you read about "Game Warden Eddy" and Irishman Dan McEachern, whose logging crew included thirty-two lumberjacks and four women cooks. At 0.7 mile, the trail crosses a stream and enters what's left of the clearing that surrounded Tyoga, a town that included not only the mill but a company store, a cook shanty capable of seating up to forty men at once, a boardinghouse, and ten private homes where lumberjacks paid twenty-five cents a day to stay, laundry service included.

The railroad grade is at post number 12, and at one time you could board a Duluth–South Shore and Atlantic train here for a trip to Detroit, Buffalo, and Cleveland. Price of a one-way ticket back then: six dollars and fifty cents. You cross another gurgling stream, learn that the white pine was 5 feet in diameter and 150 feet tall when the loggers cut the trees, and at post number 16 read about the children of Tyoga. During the summers, the youngsters fished for brook trout that often weighed up to three and a half pounds. They knew the best time to catch the trout was when the dam was open to let the water out for a log drive. Then they would take a wheelbarrow and, according to the

The start of the Tyoga Historic Pathway

interpretive sign, "pick up the trout that were left high and dry."

You recross the Laughing Fish River at 1.2 miles and pass five more interpretive signs, covering everything from popular hunting weapons of the day to a pack of timber wolves that once roamed the area, before returning to the trailhead.

65 IRONJAW SEMI-PRIMITIVE AREA

Location ■	Hiawatha National Forest
County ■	Alger
Type ■	Overnight
Difficulty ■	Easy
Hikable ■	May to November
Length ■	2 miles, round trip
Fee ■	None
Information ■	Manistique Ranger District, 906-341-5666

There are two surprises at the end of the trail to Rumble Lake in Ironjaw Semi-Primitive Area. The first is the lake itself: small and serene, with a shoreline unburdened by cottages or docks. It's the reason you drive six hours to the Upper Peninsula.

The other is the shelter overlooking the lake. Even if you know it's there, you'll be pleasantly surprised when you reach it. The Adirondack-style shelter is positioned so that a view of the lake fills its open side while the back wall will protect you from any sudden blows out of the north.

Part of Hiawatha National Forest, Ironjaw Semi-Primitive Area is a 15-square-mile tract on the south side of the Indian River that also includes a dozen lakes of various sizes and shapes. It's semi-primitive because seven forest roads that are open to vehicles penetrate the area to provide anglers access to the various lakes. But the rest of the tract can only be accessed by Pine Marten Run, a 26-mile trail system open to hikers, equestrians, and mountain bikers. The hike described here is part of the Pine Marten Run system.

Before heading north, check with the Manistique Ranger District to make sure you're not going to be there during blackfly season (mid- to late May), a horrible time to be camping in the Upper Peninsula.

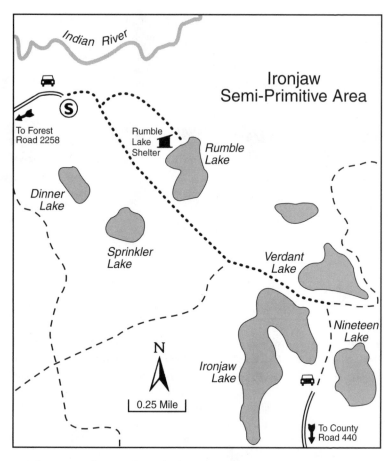

There are three Adirondack-style shelters in the Ironjaw Semi-Primitive Area. All are available on a first-come, first-served basis, no permit necessary. The one at Rumble Lake is not only snug but near, less than a mile from the trailhead, making it the ideal destination for a child's first backpacking adventure. The kids don't have to walk as far, and you, minus the tent and groundcloth, don't have to carry as much in. This is as easy as backpacking gets for a family.

To reach the trailhead from Munising, head south on H-13 for 17 miles, east on Country Road 440 for 4 miles, and north on Forest Road 2258 for 2 miles. Just before the bridge over the Indian River is a parking area and display map on the west side of FR-2258. A forest road on the east side leads 1 mile in to a vehicle-barrier gate and the start of the trail.

Park the car near the vehicle gate and follow the wide path that heads south into the stand of pines. Within 0.3 mile you reach a well-posted spur to Rumble Lake. Follow this side trail, and in less than 0.5 mile you'll be at your home-away-from-home.

Such a quick trip in means you can spend most of the afternoon exploring the area, with little more than a water bottle and lunch in your pack. Backtrack to the main trail and continue south. Within 1.5 miles you will reach the scenic heart of the tract where five lakes are clustered

Wild blackberries

close together. Here the main trail follows the crest of a ridge to provide a view of two lakes, Ironjaw and Verdant. This is the perfect lunch spot.

Return to Rumble Lake where you can finish the day listening to a campfire crackle while watching the local beaver swim back and forth across the small lake.

66 OVERLOOK TRAIL

Location ■	Fayette State Park
County ■	Delta
Type ■	Day hike
Difficulty ■	Easy
Hikable ■	May to November
Length ■	1.5 miles
Fee ■	Vehicle entry fee
Information ■	Fayette State Park headquarters, 906-644-2603

My family loves a good ghost. We're so haunted by them that the first time we visited Fayette State Park in the Upper Peninsula we

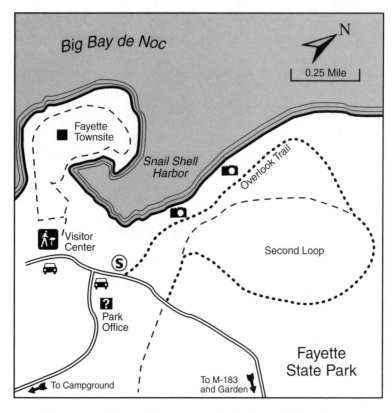

were like most visitors: We never made it beyond the ghost town. We spent the day inspecting the opera house, hotel, and other buildings of Fayette, an iron-smelting company town that was abandoned in the 1890s and eventually was restored as the historic centerpiece of this 711-acre state park.

It wasn't until our second trip that we were finally able to pull ourselves away from the ghost town to explore the park's trail system. Fayette's hiking trails consist of four loops that total 7 miles. The Overlook Trail is the shortest, at 1.5 miles, but unquestionably the most scenic. Three times along this trail you enjoy "overlooks" of beautiful Snail Shell Harbor.

The short trek combined with a visit to the park's visitor center and a stroll through the ghost town is a full afternoon for most families. Or you can stay overnight by pitching a tent or parking a trailer in the park's eighty-site campground.

To reach Fayette State Park from US-2, turn south on M-183 onto the Garden Peninsula. The town of Garden is reached in 9 miles and the first entrance to the state park in 16 miles.

Begin at the visitor center. At its height some 500 people lived, worked, and enjoyed a good life in Fayette. The town featured not only a furnace complex and numerous charcoal kilns, but also baseball fields, a hotel, even an opera house. The interpretive center has exhibits and displays devoted to the creation and downfall of the town. The heart of the museum is a scale model of Fayette as it was in the late 1880s. Although you can hike the trail and visit the town any time of the year, the visitor center and buildings are open from mid-May to mid-October daily from 9:00 A.M. to 7:00 P.M.

The Overlook Trail is located just up the road from the visitor center's parking lot. The trail begins in the woods but immediately enters a clearing. A century ago the Jackson Iron Company maintained a massive hay barn here for its sixty teams of horses and five yoke of oxen. Even more impressive than the rubbled remains, however, is the first view just around the corner. The Overlook Trail follows the limestone bluffs above Snail Shell Harbor, and whenever the trees thin out you're rewarded with a view of the historic townsite.

Within 0.25 mile of the first viewing point you reach the second overlook. This is the best spot to sit and gaze, a panorama of the entire town. You're so close to the edge of the steep-sided bluff that the park has erected a stone fence to keep little viewers on the bluff.

The ghost town of Fayette

The third overlook is reached shortly and is well beyond the harbor. From here you see across Big Bay de Noc on a clear day to the shore of the Stonington Peninsula 10 miles away on the west side.

The views from the limestone bluffs are good—so good that it's easy to miss the impressive rock outcroppings that border the trail to the east. In less than a mile from the road, the trail swings into a second-growth hardwood forest and you climb gently to a junction between the Overlook Trail and the second loop.

Head left to continue following the second loop in a clockwise direction. The last leg of the hike is a level walk in the woods along the back side of the second loop. Within 0.5 mile you arrive at a second junction, where you head left to reach the road just east of where you began.

67 NINGA AKI PATHWAY

Location ▪	Lake Superior State Forest
County ▪	Delta
Type ▪	Day hike
Difficulty ▪	Easy
Hikable ▪	May to November
Length ▪	1.5 to 2.2 miles
Fee ▪	Camping fee
Information ▪	Shingleton office, Department of Natural Resources, 906-452-6227

Located on the east side of the Upper Peninsula's Garden Peninsula in Lake Superior State Forest is Portage Bay, one of Michigan's most secluded shoreline campgrounds. The state forest campground lies on a crescent beach that is lined by pines and enclosed by a pair of rocky points at each end. The twenty-four sites are well hidden among the towering red and white pines and only three steps from the sandy beach and clear waters of Lake Michigan.

This is a rustic campground—vault toilets, hand pump for water, fire rings, and picnic tables—but such facilities only enhance the experience of spending a night at this remote bay.

Departing from the campsite area is the Ninga Aki Pathway, a 2.2-mile network of trails. The 1.5-mile Lake Michigan Loop is marked by a display sign at the north end of the campground. Bog Lake Loop is a 0.75-mile side trail. Ninga Aki is Ojibway for "Mother Earth," and posts along the trail point out the staples of the Indians' lives here when they lived off the land. Unfortunately, there are rarely any interpretive guides available at the trailhead.

This adventure begins before you even reach the campground. From the town of Garden in the middle of the peninsula, head south on County Road 483 for 2 miles to the junction known as Devils Corner. Curve to the west, and you'll head for Fayette State Park (see Hike 66). For Portage Bay continue straight on the gravel road posted "state forest campground." Turn left on Lane 12.75, and then hang on: the rugged dirt road bumps and grinds for 5 miles on its way to the east shore. First you'll pass a Department of Natural Resources boat launch and then arrive at the campground entrance, seemingly in the middle of nowhere. There

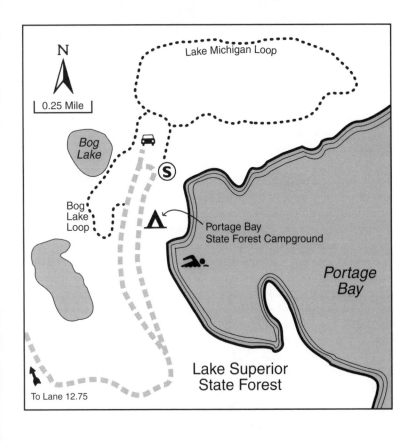

N

0.25 Mile

Lake Michigan Loop

Bog Lake

S

Bog Lake Loop

Portage Bay State Forest Campground

Portage Bay

Lake Superior State Forest

To Lane 12.75

Pink lady's slippers along Ninga Aki Pathway at Portage Bay Campground

is a nightly camping fee but no fee if you are just a day visitor.

Lake Michigan Loop is posted next to campsite number 1. The first segment of the trail is in a stand of tamarack that can be wet in early summer, but extensive boardwalks keep you out of the muddiest sections. You immediately pass post number 1 which points out juniper berries (Indians used to boil into a thick, soft mush), and then arrive at the junction with the return loop; head west (left). The next junction is Bog Lake Loop. Head north (right) to stay on Lake Michigan Loop. More planking is used to cross a wet area, but eventually the trail dries out as it moves into a spruce forest.

You're heading east when you pass post number 5, which points out a white spruce. Indians would soak the roots of these trees and lace birchbark canoes together with them. Post number 6, reached 0.75 mile from the beginning, is a balsam fir; balsam resin waterproofed the seams of canoes. You can hear the waves and then feel the cool Lake Michigan breeze long before you emerge at the shoreline at post number 8.

The trail reaches Portage Bay at its rocky northern end and heads south from there. It's hard to distinguish the trail at times, but for the next 0.4 mile you follow the bay's edge between the trees and the limestone shoreline. You'll pick up stretches of the trail here and there but always remain within view of the bay. At 1.3 miles from the trailhead, the loop becomes a well-defined path in the woods, crosses a footbridge over a stream, and arrives at the first junction. You can end the walk here or, if young legs are willing, extend it another mile by hiking Bog Lake Loop at the second junction.

This trail heads south and quickly crosses the end of the first bog, which contains very little open water. The hiking can get wet in some places before you come to the second pond in 0.3 mile, labeled on some maps as Charboneau Lake and Bog Lake on others. The small, scenic lake is an ideal place to look for pink lady's slipper, one of the state's most beautiful orchids. The trail continues past the lake for almost another 0.5 mile before it swings sharply east and emerges at the road at an unmarked location.

68 PENINSULA POINT NATURE TRAIL

Location ▪	Hiawatha National Forest, Stonington Peninsula
County ▪	Delta
Type ▪	Interpretive walk
Difficulty ▪	Easy
Hikable ▪	May to November
Length ▪	2.5 to 3 miles, round trip
Fee ▪	None
Information ▪	Rapid River Ranger District, 906-474-6442

There are two ways to reach Peninsula Point: you can drive to it or hike in. If you're thinking about driving, be advised that the U.S. Forest Service road for the final mile to the nineteenth-century lighthouse is a narrow, winding, and very bumpy one-lane road not recommended for recreational vehicles more than 16 feet long or 8 feet high.

At the time I was visiting the area I wasn't pulling an RV. But sitting behind me was a pair of squirmy children who had been in the car too long for their own good and my sanity. So we hiked in along the Peninsula Point Nature Trail.

The 1.5-mile path extends from the RV parking lot to a picnic area at the end of the Stonington Peninsula that includes Peninsula Point Lighthouse. The trail was built by the Boy Scouts in 1988, who also installed a number of interpretive displays. The plaques cover topics ranging from how to find trilobite fossils, to why the point is such a haven for birders, to what the effects of Lake Michigan's high water in 1986 and 1987 were on the shoreline.

When combined with a return walk on the Forest Service road, the trail makes for a 2.5-mile loop. Carry in lunch, and you can spend the better part of the afternoon at this scenic spot along Lake Michigan.

To reach the lighthouse from Rapid River, head east on US-2 to the Stonington exit. Head south 19 miles on County Road 513 to Stonington and then Forest Road 2204. The RV parking area and

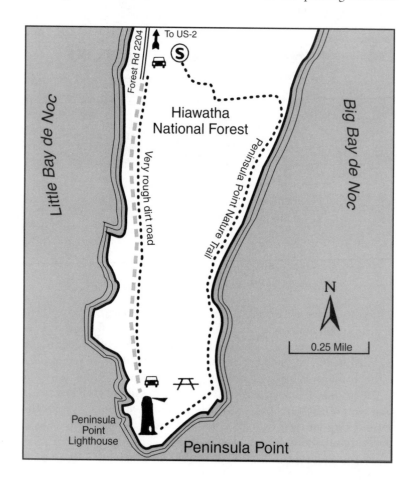

Peninsula Point Lighthouse in Hiawatha National Forest

trailhead are posted on the left just before the forest road becomes a narrow, one-lane road.

Peninsula Point Nature Trail begins in the RV parking lot and is marked by blue diamonds, which is important: Depending on what time of year you arrive, the trail can be obscured by tall grass and heavy bush in the beginning. But keep an eye out for the diamonds, and you should soon enter a cool cedar forest where it is easy to recognize the footpath.

Within 0.5 mile the trail curves sharply east, and you're rewarded with your first view of Big Bay de Noc. The remaining mile is one of the most pleasant walks in the area. For the most part the trail remains just inside the shoreline trees, providing you with shade and a constant view of the bay. You enter the open picnic area 1.5 miles from the parking lot.

The centerpiece of the day-use area is Peninsula Point Lighthouse. The U.S. Congress authorized its construction in 1864 because wooden sailing ships, hauling lumber, iron ore, and fish from Escanaba and Fayette, were no match for the treacherous shoals and reefs that separated Big Bay de Noc from Little Bay de Noc.

The structure was built in 1865 and consisted of a 40-foot tower, lit by an oil lamp and reflectors, along with an adjoining home for the lightkeeper and his family. The light went out for the last time in 1936, but the view from the point was so spectacular that the U.S. Forest Service made it into a public picnic area in 1937. The adjoining light-keeper's house burned to the ground in 1959, but the Forest Service repaired and restored the tower three years later.

Climb the forty steps to the top of the square brick tower, and you're greeted with a 360-degree panorama that includes Escanaba State Forest to the west, the limestone bluffs of Fayette State Park to the east, and the length of Lake Michigan in front of you. Surrounding the tower are picnic tables, grills, and vault toilets.

To return to the parking lot you can either rehike the trail (1.5 miles) or follow the narrow road back (1 mile).

Opposite: *A waterfall along the Canyon Gorge Trail*

WESTERN UPPER
PENINSULA

69 SUGARLOAF RECREATION TRAIL

Location ■ Little Presque Isle State Forest Recreation Area
County ■ Marquette
Type ■ Day hike
Difficulty ■ Easy
Hikable ■ May to November
Length ■ 1.2 miles, round trip
Fee ■ None
Information ■ Marquette County Visitors and Convention Bureau, 800-544-4321

Heading south on County Road 550 after a day of mountain biking in Big Bay, I asked my son if he remembered climbing Sugarloaf Mountain when he was only five. "No," he said.

There was a long pause, and he could sense my I-Don't-Know-Why-I-Bother-To-Take-You-Anywhere disappointment. "Aww come

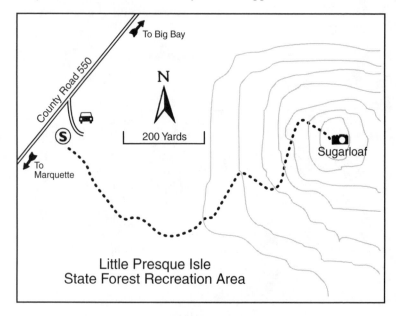

Observation area at the top of Sugarloaf near Marquette

on," he said breaking the silence, "you know how many hikes you've taken me on?"

I quickly pulled into the trailhead parking lot. Sugarloaf is one worth remembering. The mountain is really a prominent granite and gneiss knob on the edge of the Little Presque Isle State Forest Recreation Area and just north of the Upper Peninsula's largest city. For many local children—and my son as well—it's the first "mountain" they ever climb.

That's because the hike combines a pleasant walk along a wooded path, a little climbing, and a peak at the end with a glorious 360-degree view of the surrounding countryside and Lake Superior. Although there are numerous stairs to climb, this short trail can be managed even by three- and four-year-olds when plenty of rest stops are taken.

The trail is located 5 miles north of the city. Head out of Marquette on County Road 550, the road to Big Bay, and look for a dirt parking lot and a large Sugarloaf sign on the east side. This is an excellent lunchtime trail, so pack along some sandwiches and enjoy a picnic while viewing the Lake Superior shoreline. Bring something to drink, though, because there is no water along the way.

The trail begins as a wide and level path through the forest, but within 0.25 mile you reach a bench and begin climbing on an imposing stairway. The trail levels out briefly and then the wooden steps resume. There are almost 400 steps before you reach the backside of

Sugarloaf, a climb of 315 feet from the parking lot. You break out of the trees at a rounded knob marked by a stone monument and three observation decks.

The top of the 1075-foot peak provides one of the best vistas of the area, affording fine views in every direction. From the first deck you can see the Lake Superior shoreline extending south and the massive iron ore docks jutting out from the city harbors. The second deck positions you to gaze east toward the vast expanse of water that is the world's largest inland lake. From the last deck you look west onto miles of unbroken forest crowned in the center by the rocky knob known as Hogsback Mountain.

70 PIERS GORGE TRAIL

Location ▪	Piers Gorge Scenic Area
County ▪	Dickinson
Type ▪	Day hike
Difficulty ▪	Moderate
Hikable ▪	May to November
Length ▪	3 miles, round trip
Fee ▪	None
Information ▪	Tourism Association of Dickinson County, 906-774-2945 or 800-236-2447; Kosir's Rapid Rafts, 715-757-3431

Michigan's wildest white water is the stretch of the Menominee River that flows through Piers Gorge, 2 miles south of Norway on the state border with Wisconsin. Here the river has sliced through bedrock to form an area of holes, hydraulics, swirls, and a 10-foot drop known to rafters and kayakers as "Misicot."

During the summer the hike offers an impressive display of white-water rafting, especially if you arrive on Saturday or Sunday afternoon when local rafting companies are running trips through the gorge. To sit on the edge of the gorge and watch rubber rafts crash into swirls of white water is exciting for children and adults alike.

The area is reached by heading south of Norway on US-8. Just before crossing the bridge to the Wisconsin side of the Menominee River, a sign for the Piers Gorge Scenic Area directs you to turn right

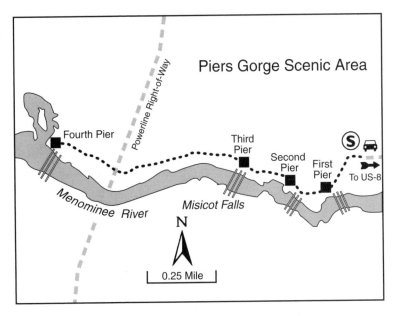

Piers Gorge Scenic Area

Fourth Pier

Third Pier

Second Pier

First Pier

Powerline Right-of-Way

Menominee River

Misicot Falls

To US-8

N

0.25 Mile

(west). The paved road quickly becomes dirt, at which point you veer left. In 0.5 mile it ends at a parking area with a large display map.

Piers Gorge picked up its name from the wooden piers that lumber companies built in the river here to slow the current and thus the logs they were floating to mills on Lake Michigan. There are four piers signposts along the trail; each marks a spur to a stretch of the river's spectacular white water. From the parking lot, a wood-chip trail heads west and quickly crosses a footbridge, and at 0.2 mile arrives at the First Pier. The spur here leads you to a mild stretch of rapids.

The trail continues west and makes its first climb. You top off at the Second Pier, a spot where the white water is much more intense. From here the trail climbs again and this time you top off at the Third Pier, 0.5 mile from the trailhead. Below is Misicot Falls, a mesmerizing 10-foot drop in the river. Here you stand on the rocky edge of the canyon and watch water crash through this vicious stretch of holes, falls, and whirlpools. If there are any rafters on the river, this is where you want to watch them.

The trail stays in sight of the white water for a little longer and then at 0.8 mile swings away from the river to become a shady and quiet walk in the forest. At 1 mile you emerge at the powerline right-of-way and then reenter the forest on the other side to come to a V junction. Blue diamonds lead you down the right fork to the Fourth Pier, the

beginning of the white water.

The Fourth Pier falls is a one-way hike of 1.5 miles and makes for a good spot to turn around or to enjoy lunch before turning around. To the west the river is calm, while to the east it's entering its first rock chute. Between the two, a small rock spit sticks out into the river, where more than one young hiker has soaked tired feet before heading back.

For those wanting to experience the rapids, not just view them, the Wisconsin rafting company Kosir's Rapid Rafts (phone 715-757-3431) runs this stretch throughout the summer.

The white water at Piers Gorge attracts kayakers and rafters from around the Midwest.

71 CANYON GORGE TRAIL

Location ▪	Canyon Falls Roadside Area
County ▪	Baraga
Type ▪	Day hike
Difficulty ▪	Easy
Hikable ▪	May to November
Length ▪	1 to 2 miles, round trip
Fee ▪	None
Information ▪	Baraga County Tourist and Recreation Association, 906-524-7444

Not all rest areas consist of picnic tables, trash cans, and a pair of vault toilets. A Michigan Department of Transportation roadside park on US-41 also serves as the trailhead to a beautiful falls and a stunning rock canyon, the largest box canyon in the state. On that long drive across the Upper Peninsula, Canyon Falls Roadside Area lets children and their parents stretch their legs by undertaking an easy 1- to 2-mile hike before continuing on.

The roadside park is on the west side of US-41, 8 miles south of

L'Anse or 60 miles west of Marquette. The Department of Transportation maintains the rest area, but it was forestry students from Michigan Technological University who built the path and constructed the wooden boardwalks and observation platforms that make this trek such an easy and enjoyable one.

From the large display of the trail in the rest area, the path leads into the woods and immediately comes to a junction at an interpretive area devoted to the multiple-use concept of forests. The trail to Canyon Falls continues on as the left-hand fork, crossing a bridge over Bacco Stream.

Within 0.3 mile you swing by the cola-colored Sturgeon River and arrive at the first falls, a cascade with about a 2-foot drop. Occasionally somebody thinks this is Canyon Falls, but there is no mistaking the real one, which is just another 0.2 mile down the trail. Canyon Falls has an impressive 20-foot drop and marks the beginning of the gorge, which extends west another 0.5 mile along the river. Guardrails have been erected at this point and allow you to lean over the top of the cascade and feel the mist the falling water creates.

At this point there is a "Trail Ends" sign. But the best part of the area is the gorge itself, and the original path can be seen snaking around the huge rock face where the sign is posted. It hugs the gorge and allows you to peer down between the sheer walls of rock to more white water below.

Everybody, especially families with young children, should be

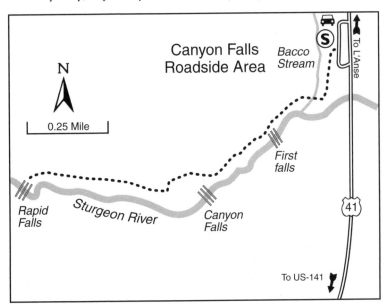

Canyon Falls

 extremely careful if they choose to continue to the end of the old trail, for a total one-way hike of a mile to Rapid Falls. The original log guardrails are still up but flimsy and weak in places, and after they end there is nothing between you and the sharp edge of the gorge. But Canyon Gorge is one of the most beautiful chasms in Michigan, and a careful walk along the path rewards you with a fascinating view of glacially sculptured rock formations.

From Canyon Falls, the original path continues another 0.5 mile until it emerges from the gorge and descends to the river's edge just beyond Rapid Falls. From here you backtrack both the old trail and the maintained one to return to the rest area.

72 LITTLE MOUNTAIN TRAIL

Location	Little Mountain, Town of L'Anse
County	Baraga
Type	Day hike
Difficulty	Moderate
Hikable	May to November
Length	2.5 miles, round trip
Fee	None
Information	Baraga County Tourist and Recreation Association, 906-524-7444

Little Mountain Trail is a round-trip hike of 2.5 miles to the top of a 1155-foot-high rocky bluff with spectacular views. For years this was an obscure trail and overlook that only locals knew about and could find. But in 2000 the Baraga Tourist and Recreation Association erected better signs at the trailhead and along the path, and now it's a delightful hike for families . . . even those who don't live in L'Anse.

Start the day out at the Hilltop Restaurant in L'Anse, where you can indulge in its famous sweet rolls that are five inches high, three inches across, and arrive at your table dripping in a sugary glaze. Then burn off that breakfast feast by hiking Canyon Gorge (see Hike 71) and then Little Mountain.

To reach Little Mountain from L'Anse, head south on US-41 for 5 miles to Golf Course Road, located next to Tony's Steak Shop. Turn right (west) on Golf Course Road and follow it to the end, where there is a small parking area marked by large boulders that have been painted white, and a trail sign for Little Mountain.

From the parking lot a path continues west into the woods and quickly crosses a footbridge over a small stream. In less than a mile from the trailhead you'll pass a weathered sign for Little Mountain Trail and then swing south toward a rocky ridge.

At the ridge the trail swings west again around the base and then curves back east to ascend Little Mountain's back side. The climb can be steep at times but is a short one. Within 0.25 mile of climbing you break out of the pines to a rounded, rocky knob, the peak.

From the top of Little Mountain there is a very big view. It's as spectacular as any high point we have climbed in Michigan, even the Lake of the Clouds Escarpment in the Porcupine Mountains or Avalanche Peak overlooking Lake Charlevoix (see Hike 54).

To the north the towns of L'Anse and Baraga are at your feet, Keweenaw Bay just beyond them, and on the horizon is Brockway

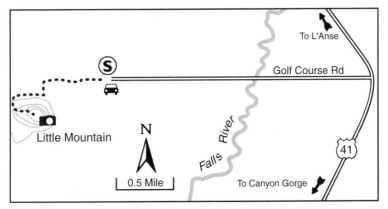

Mountain, the backbone of the Keweenaw Peninsula. To the southwest you stare at the rugged terrain and unbroken forests that stretch into the Sturgeon River Gorge Wilderness (see Hike 74).

But the best views are to the east. Here you can sit on the edge of a large, square boulder and gaze at the roof of Michigan: the Huron Mountains. The tallest peak, in the center, is Mount Arvon, the highest point in Michigan at 1979 feet.

73 TIP TRAIL

Location ■	Point Abbaye Natural Area
County ■	Baraga
Type ■	Day hike
Difficulty ■	Easy
Hikable ■	May to November
Length ■	1.3 miles
Fee ■	None
Information ■	Baraga County Tourist and Recreation Association, 906-524-7444

Sometimes my children and I are drawn to a place because a campground is there or a hiking trail or maybe a fishing pier on a lake

Enjoying the view at Point Abbaye Natural Area

where we can catch bluegill. And sometimes we go just because it's the end of the road. Point Abbaye is a place at the end of the road.

We've stared at it for years on a map of Michigan, knowing only that it's the tip of the long peninsula that separates Lake Superior's Keweenaw Bay from Huron Bay in the Upper Peninsula. There was no state park there, no national forest campground, no nature center. There might not even be a view here, though somehow I suspected there was.

Finally one afternoon while we were in Baraga County we drove to the end of that road and discovered that the tip was preserved as the Point Abbaye Natural Area, containing trails, unusual rock formations, and panoramic views.

Surprise, surprise.

The point is a 23-mile drive from L'Anse. From US-41/M-28 head north on Main Street, which outside of L'Anse turns into Skanee Road. Skanee heads north, then east where it crosses the Silver River. Turn north (left) on Townline Road, the first junction after Silver River, then east (right) on Point Abbaye Road.

The last 10 miles of the drive along Point Abbaye Road is a winding dirt road that's probably impassable after a heavy rain. It's the kind of road that in 10 minutes makes your vehicle look like it's just returned from a month-long African safari.

At the end of the road is a sign welcoming you to Point Abbaye Natural Area, a small parking area, and a pair of pit toilets. The small natural area contains three short paths—Tip Trail, Woods Trail, and Bay Trail—that can be combined into a single loop of 1.3 miles.

Tip Trail leaves the parking lot as a two-track and is marked by a series of large boulders to prevent people from driving out to the

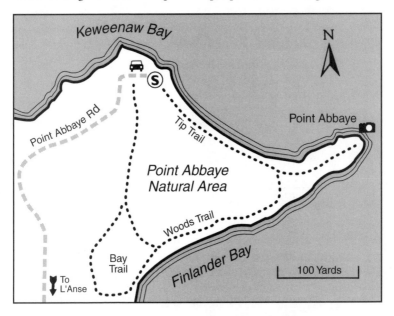

point. It's a level walk through a pleasant forest of maple, beech, and birch, but within a few steps water appears through the trees on both sides of you. Within 0.4 mile from the parking lot you emerge from the brush at the tip.

The views from Point Abbaye are stunning, perhaps one of Michigan's best panoramas. To the north is the outline of Brockway Mountain on the Keweenaw Peninsula. To the southeast are the Huron Mountains. Due south is the Huron River emptying into Lake Superior, and due east are the Huron Islands, rocky islets that have sunk more than their share of ships.

There are unique rock formations to explore at the point. The shoreline here is reddish rock that has been carved into graceful curves and smooth dips during Lake Superior's temperamental moods. The area also abounds with thimbleberries, a sweet berry that is found in few other places in Michigan other than the western Upper Peninsula.

To return, backtrack on Tip Trail to the junction with Woods Trail and head south (left). Keep an eye out for the orange diamonds that mark the path, as both Woods and Bay Trails can be obscure at times. You skirt the shoreline of Finlander Bay for 0.4 mile and then swing inland to arrive at a posted junction. Head left again. Bay Trail is 0.3 mile long and continues along Finlander Bay before looping back through the forest to Woods Trail, just south of the parking lot.

74 STURGEON FALLS TRAIL

Location ■	Sturgeon River Gorge Wilderness
County ■	Houghton
Type ■	Day hike or overnight
Difficulty ■	Moderate to challenging
Hikable ■	May to November
Length ■	1.5 miles, round trip
Fee ■	None
Information ■	Kenton Ranger District office, 906-852-3500

Split between Baraga and Houghton Counties, Sturgeon River Gorge Wilderness is a 14,139-acre tract in Ottawa National Forest. This is perhaps one of the most remote and rugged areas in Michigan. In places the

Sturgeon and Little Silver Rivers have carved the wilderness into steep-sided gorges 300 feet deep and up to a mile wide.

Luckily, the area's most impressive natural attraction—Sturgeon Falls—is also the most accessible and makes for a great day hike with children. Although the trail is a round trip of only 1.5 miles, it does involve a steep descent and climb out of the Sturgeon Gorge. Switchbacks in the trail make this trek considerably easier, but this can still be a challenging hike for young children.

Haul in a tent and sleeping bags, and you can turn the hike into an overnight adventure. It's possible to set up camp so close to the falls

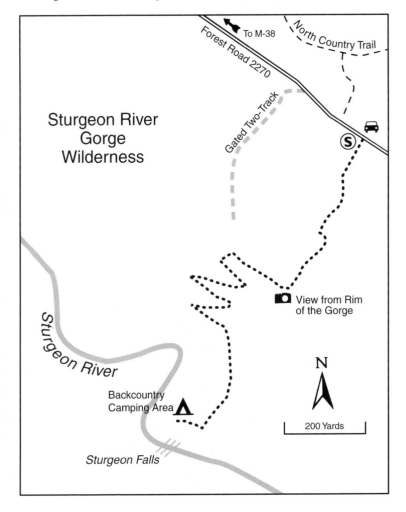

that at night the cascading water will lull you to sleep and then permeate your dreams.

From Baraga, head west on M-38 for 10 miles and then turn south (left) on Prickett Dam Road. Within 3 miles veer right on Forest Road 2270, passing the access road to Silver Mountain in another 3 miles. From here you descend to cross the Sturgeon River on a bridge, climb back to the rim of the gorge, and continue another 2 miles along FR 2270. Within 10 miles of M-38 you will arrive at a small parking area on the east side of the road and a large sign marking the trailhead for Sturgeon Falls Trail on the west side.

From the trailhead you head southwest along a level trail through a mixed forest of pines, hemlock, and hardwoods such as maples and some birch. Within 0.2 mile you arrive at the rim of the gorge where the trail swings north and follows it briefly. If it's autumn and the leaves have begun to drop, you'll be rewarded with glimpse of the rugged interior of the Sturgeon River Gorge Wilderness to the west.

Sturgeon Falls in Sturgeon River Gorge Wilderness

Eventually the trail swings west and drops into the gorge. For more than 0.3 mile you follow a series of switchbacks that make the steep descent much more manageable. The trail eventually levels out and then, 0.75 mile from the trailhead, arrives at a flat area within view of the river. This is a popular place to set up camp.

Numerous trails in the area will descend to various viewing points of the Sturgeon River. One is of the river upstream before rock walls and outcroppings constrict at the falls. Another path leads you to where the current roars through a narrow chute. The last is the most impressive, as it puts you near the base of Sturgeon Falls where the river drops more than 30 feet into a sea of foam. The steep rock walls of the Sturgeon Gorge are all around you, while downstream is a stranded pile of tree trunks and roots, a testimony to the river's power and velocity during the high water of spring.

75 NORWAY LAKE TRAIL

Location ■	Ottawa National Forest
County ■	Iron
Type ■	Interpretive walk or overnight
Difficulty ■	Easy
Hikable ■	May to November
Length ■	1.2 miles
Fee ■	None
Information ■	Kenton Ranger District office, 906-852-3500

Easy backpacking? Some people think that's an oxymoron. How can carrying anything on your back, much less a portable household, ever be easy?

But the secret to easing children into backpacking is not in limiting what they carry—heck, you'll be carrying most of the equipment anyhow—but carefully planning where they are walking. You want a trail that is short but interesting with a backcountry campsite that is secluded but nearby. You want to lead them away from the car to a spot where it's fun to spend the night without any facilities . . . not even a bathroom.

Now, that's a challenge—but there are dozens of such spots throughout Michigan, and Norway Lake Trail is one of them. This short loop features a pair of walk-in sites, so you can take children as young as four or five years old "backpacking" if you're willing to carry a couple of extra sleeping bags.

Part of Ottawa National Forest in the Upper Peninsula's Iron County, Norway Lake Trail is located on the narrow strip of land that separates its namesake lake to the east from Nesbit Lake to the west. On Norway Lake there is a delightful national forest campground, on Nesbit Lake there is a summer youth camp on the west shore, and in between the two is this 1.2-mile nature trail.

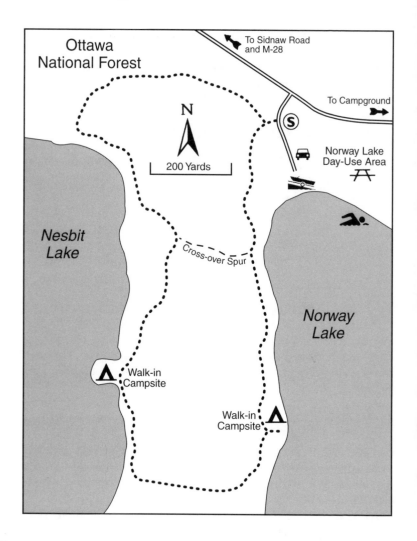

 To reach Norway Lake from M-28 in Sidnaw, head south on Sidnaw Road for 6 miles. Turn west on Forest Road 2400, and you'll reach Norway Lake Campground in 2 miles. If you are planning an overnight trek, either pack in drinking water or carry a filter; there is no drinking water at the sites.

The trail departs from the Norway Lake Campground boat launch, and the first half is an easy but scenic walk along the lakeshore. The nature trail features fifteen interpretive posts that examine everything from deer trails and a bog where you can look for pitcher plants, to a huge pine that was snapped in half by a single bolt of lighting.

But the best part of this short trail is its pair of walk-in campsites, one on each lake. The first, less than 0.5 mile from the trailhead, offers absolutely no facilities, but the site is a level spot in a stand of red pine where one morning we enjoyed our Captain Crunch cereal while watching small bass rise.

At this point the trail swings away from Norway Lake and cuts over to Nesbit Lake, west and north to the second campsite, 0.7 mile from the trailhead. This one is delightful. It's situated on a small peninsula on the east side of the lake, a spot that usually catches enough wind to keep the bugs at bay.

The site is not very big and it's not very level, but there is more than enough room for a small tent that can be pitched only a few feet from the water. If there is no group at the youth camp, you'll virtually have the lake to yourself.

From the campsite, the trail continues north and slightly inland away from the shore of Nesbit Lake. You return to a view of the water within 0.3 mile and then the trail swings east, passing the last two interpretive signs and arriving at the boat launch to complete the 1.2-mile loop.

76 BEAVER LODGE TRAIL

Location ■ Ottawa National Forest
County ■ Houghton
Type ■ Interpretive walk
Difficulty ■ Easy to moderate
Hikable ■ May to November
Length ■ 1.25 miles
Fee ■ Camping fee
Information ■ Kenton Ranger District office,
906-852-3500

Bob Lake Campground is a pleasant facility on an undeveloped and somewhat remote lake in Ottawa National Forest. Like most U.S. Forest Service campgrounds, Bob Lake is rustic, featuring vault toilets and sites that are well spread out in a heavily forested area. Unlike many campgrounds, Bob Lake offers a range of hiking opportunities.

Departing from the campground's day-use area is Beaver Lodge Trail. This 1.25-mile loop passes twenty interpretive plaques and two active beaver ponds, providing children with both a natural history lesson and an opportunity to spot wildlife. Not long enough? A spur connects Beaver Lodge Trail to the North Country Trail, which passes through the area. Once on the North Country Trail you can hike all day if the kids are up to it. For more information on this long-distance trail, contact the North Country Trail Association (phone 616-454-5506).

The campground has twenty-six sites on a single loop, with six of them directly on the lakeshore. Facilities include tables, fire rings with sliding grills, and lantern posts. Nearby is the day-use area with a small beach and swimming area along with picnic tables, grills, and changing rooms.

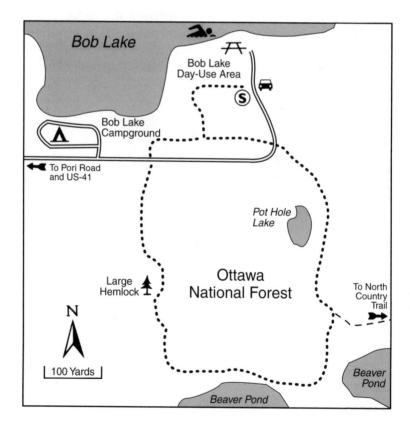

The campground is reached from US-41, 30 miles east of L'Anse. Drive south on Forest Highway 16 for 5 miles and then west (right) on Pori Road for 2 miles. Turn south (left) onto Forest Highway 1470, and in 2 miles you'll reach the campground. There is no fee for parking in the day-use area and hiking the trails. There is a per-site fee if you decide to spend the night.

Beaver Lodge Trail begins in the day-use parking lot. Within the first few minutes you pass a floating bog on the edge of Bob Lake, cross the campground road, and then begin climbing a ridge via a stairway. At the top is a bench and a display board with a sign announcing "This Is Bear Country!" That ought to make a few kids look nervously around.

You then skirt a small, marshy pond that an interpretive plaque explains is a "pot hole lake," and descend to the spur to the North Country Trail, 0.5 mile from the trailhead. Head right (south) at this junction, and you will soon arrive at a flooded beaver pond. At the far end is the lodge, while all around the shore are dead trees. Three interpretive plaques explain how a pair of beavers, by damming one small stream, have drastically changed acres of terrain. A bench allows you to sit for a spell in hopes of seeing the beavers at work.

The trail crosses the stream, and from the middle of the bridge you are within full view of a massive beaver dam. A few minutes from the first beaver pond you arrive at a second one. This pond is considerably larger and features another lodge. The trail passes several places along the shore where you can sit and look for wildlife.

During the summer beavers are constantly working to improve their lodge, repair the dam, and cache their winter food supply, usually aspen branches whose succulent bark tides them over to spring. You can see signs of beavers along the trail, trees they have cut down and their paths down to the water. Or, arrive at dusk or dawn and spend some time quietly observing the surface of the ponds. Eventually you'll spot a beaver swimming steadily past you.

At 0.75 miles, the trail swings away from the second pond and climbs the ridge, topping off at a stand of large hemlock where deer often gather during the winter for shelter. You follow the rolling ridge for another 0.25 mile and then descend to the campground road. On the other side the trail merges into an old logging railroad bed that dates back to the early 1900s and still features a few of the original ties. Head right to return to the day-use area.

77 CASCADE FALLS TRAIL

Location ▪ Ottawa National Forest
County ▪ Ontonagon
Type ▪ Day hike
Difficulty ▪ Moderate
Hikable ▪ May to November
Length ▪ 1.8-mile loop
Fee ▪ None
Information ▪ Bergland District office, 906-575-3441

Cascade Falls Trail is a 1.8-mile loop to just one of the Upper Peninsula's many waterfalls. The cascading water is scenic but not as spectacular as Tahquamenon Falls (Hike 61) or those seen along Black River Drive (Hike 80). What makes this adventure unique and a delight to many children is not the falls but the peaks. Along the Twin Peaks Route of the loop kids climb the side of a rocky ridge to arrive at something of a summit, with a sweeping view of the Trap Hills off in the distance. They do this not once but twice.

The steep climbs are the reason for the moderate rating despite the trail's short length. Children under five or six might have trouble with the Twin Peaks Route, in which case they should stay on the Valley Route, a shorter and considerably easier lowland walk to the falls. Everybody should be wearing boots, especially when hiking over the rocky terrain to the peaks.

From the Forest Service district office in Bergland, head east on

Cascade Falls in Ottawa National Forest

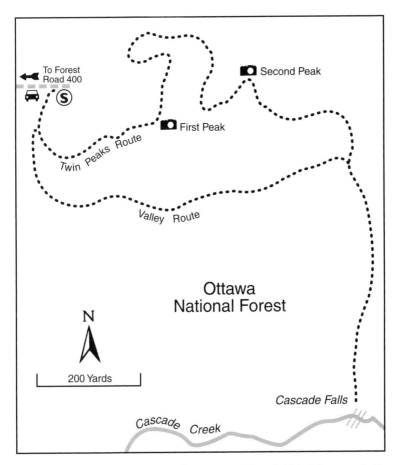

M-28 for 1 mile and then north on Forest Road 400. It's a scenic 7-mile drive along the dirt road into the heart of Ottawa National Forest before you cross a bridge over Cascade Creek and are directed by a sign to turn right for the trailhead.

If you are planning to hike the entire loop, it's best to start right off with the Twin Peaks Route, while legs are still fresh. The trail is well posted and begins with an immediate ascent toward the top of a rocky bluff. At times it may be difficult to see the path, but in 0.2 mile you should arrive at the first peak, an opening where to the west you see the rugged Trap Hills, while down below is Cascade Creek and the West Branch of the Ontonagon River.

The view is nice, but tell the troops it's time to climb the next peak. The trail cuts through a stand of oak, aspen, and hemlock and then resumes climbing. In another quarter mile you reach the second high point, with more good views of the Upper Peninsula's rugged interior and possibly Lake Gogebic to the south. From here it's a rapid descent that levels out somewhat before merging with the Valley Route.

It's only 0.3 mile to the creek. Cascade Falls are small but picturesque and are located on the creek just before it empties into the West Branch. The falls are surrounded by large rocks, where you can sit and listen to the cascading water or watch trout rise in the pool upstream before heading back.

You backtrack to the junction and then head along the Valley Route. This trail is 0.4 mile long and stays entirely in a forest of aspen, balsam, and hemlock. Look for the flat-topped stumps and other evidence of past timber-cutting activities in this area.

78 GOVERNMENT PEAK TRAIL

Location ▪	Porcupine Mountains Wilderness State Park
County ▪	Ontonagon
Type ▪	Overnight
Difficulty ▪	Challenging
Hikable ▪	June to November
Length ▪	5.2 miles, round trip
Fee ▪	Vehicle entry fee and camping fee
Information ▪	Porcupine Mountains Wilderness State Park headquarters, 906-885-5275

Quick! Before the kids have to go back to school and you have to start attending PTA meetings, grab the backpacks and a comfortable pair of hiking boots, throw in the raingear but pray for sun, and head west to the Porcupine Mountains for the last trek of the summer. Michigan's largest and most rugged state park has a wonderful trail system that winds through 60,000 acres. One of our favorite hikes in the park is an overnight trek to the Trap Falls shelter along Government Peak Trail, a one-way hike of 2.6 miles.

Government Peak Trail is actually a 7.5-mile one-way path that begins at M-107, near Lake of the Clouds Overlook, and ends in the middle of the park near Mirror Lake. But because it doesn't wind past any of the park's sixteen wilderness cabins or the shoreline of Lake Superior, the trail is not nearly as heavily used as most other routes in the park.

And by the end of the summer or early fall, you often feel like you're the only ones in the park. To us, this is the Porkies at their best: the end of the tourist season, on an isolated stretch of trail in the middle of these rugged ridges.

The park is reached from Silver City in the Upper Peninsula by continuing west on M-107. Within 2 miles you reach South Boundary Road where you can head south to the park's visitor center. All overnight hikers must register before embarking on their trek and obtain a rustic camping permit and a vehicle entry permit. Both

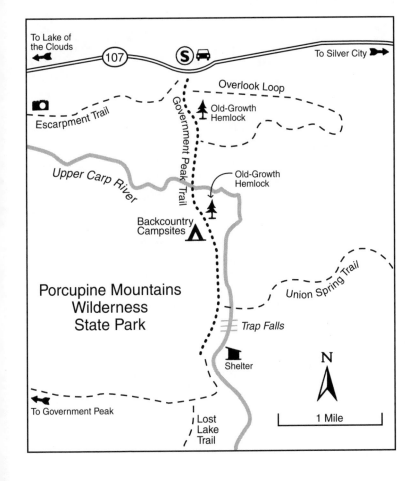

Backpackers leave a shelter at Porcupine Mountains Wilderness State Park.

backcountry campsites and the trail shelters are used on a first-come, first-served basis.

The trailhead for Government Peak Trail is posted on the south side of M-107 6 miles west of the visitor center turn-off. M-107 ends another 4 miles west at Lake of the Clouds Overlook.

From M-107, Government Peak Trail heads south and within a mile passes three junctions with the Escarpment Trail and the Over-look Loop, and then crosses the Upper Carp River. Once over the river, the scenic part begins. The trail climbs through an old-growth forest of hemlock with the Upper Carp River gurgling right along-side of you like a mountain stream. In the middle of this gorge-like area, only 1.5 miles from the trailhead, is a pair of backcountry camp-sites, each with a fire ring and a level spot for your tent overlooking the river.

Continue climbing, and 2.4 miles from M-107 you arrive at Trap Falls. The cascade is well named. The Upper Carp tumbles 15 feet down a narrow rock ledge here into a basin below that "traps" the river momentarily in a deep pool before letting it go. Pines tower over this scenic spot, and if it's the middle of the summer you might see a couple of backpackers cooling off in the pool. If it's early fall, you'll have the falls to yourself.

Continue on the trail, and 2.6 miles from the trailhead, after fording the Upper Carp, you'll reach one of the park's three Adirondack-style shelters. Each three-sided shelter is screened in on the fourth side and has a table and sleeping platforms inside.

Regardless whether you're staying in the backcountry campsites or the shelter, this is a great spot to spend an extra day. You can hike to the top of Government Peak, the second highest point in the Porkies at 1850 feet, for a round-trip walk of 5.4 miles from Trap Falls shelter. Another scenic walk is the 6-mile hike south to Lost Lake.

79 EAST AND WEST RIVER TRAILS

Location ■	Porcupine Mountains Wilderness State Park
County ■	Ontonagon
Type ■	Day hike
Difficulty ■	Moderate
Hikable ■	June to November
Length ■	2 miles, round trip
Fee ■	Vehicle entry fee
Information ■	Porcupine Mountains Wilderness State Park headquarters, 906-885-5275

East River Trail and West River Trail are actually two separate paths, but when combined (as they usually are) they form a scenic loop in the Porcupine Mountains Wilderness State Park and the best day hike for families with young children. The outing packs in adventure, stands of virgin hemlock, waterfalls, and great scenery almost every step of the way along a loop that is only 2 miles long.

The end of the Presque Isle River is one of the most spectacular spots in Michigan. In its final mile before emptying into Lake Superior, the Presque Isle descends more than 100 feet and in doing so has carved a rugged and steep-sided gorge and filled it with waterfalls.

You begin and end this hike near Presque Isle Campground on the west side of the park. The semi-modern facility has eighty-eight sites located on a bluff above Lake Superior and features modern restrooms and showers but not electric outlets for recreational vehicles.

Porcupine Mountains Wilderness State Park is 17 miles west of Ontonagon via M-64 and M-107. Once in the park, head south on

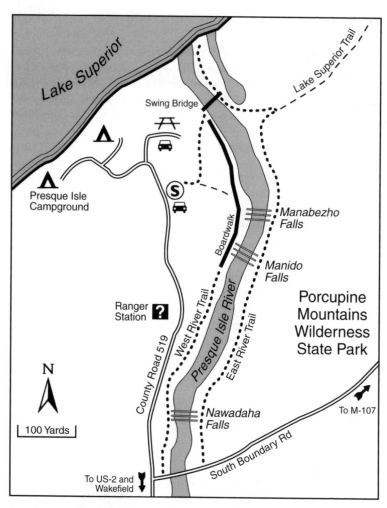

South Boundary Road and follow it until ends at County Road 519. Head north on CR 519 to reach the Presque Isle day-use area.

West River Trail begins in the day-use area and wastes no time in getting to the river. The trail immediately turns into a long stairway that leads you down to the Presque Isle River and across the rushing water on an impressive swing bridge. From the middle of the bridge, you enjoy an incredible view upstream. Presque Isle is by far the largest river to flow through the Porkies, and its current is so strong that the whirlpool swirl of the water has carved perfect half-circles in the bedrock below you. What appears on maps as a peninsula on the other side of the bridge is actually an island in the mouth of the river with a dry channel on one side.

In the middle of the island there is a spur that will lead you to within view of the rugged shoreline of Lake Superior. But this loop continues across the island to the waterless channel that is the east side of the gorge. When crossing the channel you'll actually walk over layers of shale, while in the background is a small waterfall. It's impressive scenery and fun hiking.

East River Trail begins with a steep climb out of the gorge, topping off at the posted junction with the 16-mile-long Lake Superior Trail. Then East River Trail heads south, climbing along the edge of the gorge and over masses of roots from the towering stand of virgin hemlock, white pine, and cedar.

Within 0.6 mile from the day-use area, the trail descends to a bench overlooking Manabezho and Manido Falls, a pair of thundering cascades, one just downriver from the other. You first reach 20-foot Manabezho Falls, the largest drop along the river. The falls thunder over a rock ledge and create a heavy mist and a blanket of foam. Another 100 yards upstream is Manido Falls, which descend 25 feet over a gradually declining set of rock ledges.

The trail stays on the edge of the gorge, and you can view a series of cascades for the next 0.5 mile until you arrive at Nawadaha Falls where the river tumbles 15 feet over a series of rock steps. At this point the trail swings away from the river and you break out at South Boundary Road, the halfway point in the hike.

You have barely crossed the Presque Isle River on South Boundary Road Bridge when you leave the pavement and return to a needle-carpeted path through an impressive stand of hemlock. West River Trail is an easier hike. You begin near the river and weave through the trees, passing Nawadaha Falls a

Backpacker, Porcupine Mountains Wilderness State Park

second time. Within 0.5 mile of South Boundary Road you arrive at an extensive boardwalk that puts you right above Manido Falls and then Manabezho. You're so close you can feel their cooling mist on a hot afternoon. All too soon you return to the stairway that leads back to the day-use area.

80 BLACK RIVER FALLS

Location ▪	Ottawa National Forest
County ▪	Gogebic
Type ▪	Day hike
Difficulty ▪	Easy to moderate
Hikable ▪	June to November
Length ▪	One-way trails vary from 0.2 to 0.8 mile
Fee ▪	None
Information ▪	Bessemer District Office, 906-667-0261

Perhaps more than mountains, large tracts of wilderness, or the icy waters of Lake Superior, waterfalls are the trademark of the Upper Peninsula. There are hundreds of cascades in the Upper Peninsula, as opposed to just a pair in the Lower Peninsula, and they include such well-known leaps as Tahquamenon Falls (Hike 61), the third largest east of the Mississippi, and Munising Falls, set in a rock amphitheater. But the best collection of falling white water is found along Black River Drive (also labeled CR 513) in the western end of the Upper Peninsula.

Departing from Bessemer, the paved road heads north for 15 miles to end at Black River Harbor, one of the few access points to Lake Superior and the site of an Ottawa National Forest campground. It's a scenic drive past high rocky bluffs and the rugged hills that have made Bessemer a haven for skiers during the winter. But the high point of the trip consists of five waterfalls, all located a short walk from the road.

The cascades are linked together by a portion of the North Country Trail, which hikers can walk from Cooper Peak Ski Flying Hill to the campground, a 5.5-mile trip. But it's more convenient for traveling families and more enjoyable for young children if you drive the road, stopping at the trailhead of each individual falls. The hikes are

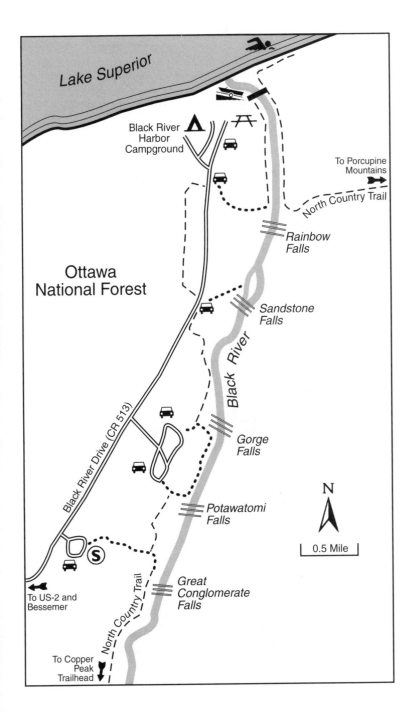

Lake Superior

Black River
Harbor
Campground

To Porcupine
Mountains

North Country Trail

Rainbow
Falls

Ottawa
National Forest

Sandstone
Falls

Black River

Gorge
Falls

N

0.5 Mile

Potawatomi
Falls

Black River Drive (CR 513)

Great
Conglomerate
Falls

To US-2 and
Bessemer

(S)

North Country Trail

To Copper
Peak
Trailhead

short, the longest being a 1.6-mile round trip, and the trails well marked and maintained. While they can be walked in tennis shoes, they do include a number of long staircases, and for that reason visiting all five falls makes for an adventure of moderate difficulty.

The first is Great Conglomerate Falls, located 12 miles north of US-2 in Bessemer. The trail is a one-way walk of 0.8 mile and begins as a level forest walk for 0.5 mile, then drops steadily to the posted junction with the North Country Trail. Near the junction is an overview of the falls, really two falls with a 40-foot total drop split in half by a huge rock face. For a little added adventure, you can send half your party north along the North Country Trail to reach the next set of cascades, Potawatomi and Gorge Falls, in 0.5 mile. The others can return to the car and drive to the next trailhead.

The posted trailhead for Potawatomi and Gorge Falls is another mile along Black River Road and marks the entrance to both falls. The best way to view them is to begin with the trail to Potawatomi Falls and then hike along the river a short way to Gorge Falls before returning to the parking area, for a 0.8-mile loop. The trail passes a junction with the North Country Trail and then emerges at a view of the Potawatomi Falls, a cascade 130 feet wide with a 30-foot drop.

Gorge Falls is only 800 feet downriver, but the trail passes five observation platforms, with the first providing the best view of

A father and son admire Rainbow Falls along Black River Drive.

Potawatomi Falls. The fourth platform, however, is the most spectacular, putting you right over the 24-foot drop of Gorge Falls and providing an excellent view of the rock canyon the Black River has carved over time. No two waterfalls are alike, and nowhere is that better seen than here. Gorge Falls is a narrow drop of thundering water, while Potawatomi is a spread-out veil flowing over a rock embankment.

It's another mile north along Black River Road to reach the posted trailhead of Sandstone Falls. The 0.2-mile trail is basically a long staircase descent to the river, where you can scramble over large red rocks to stand almost directly over the falls and feel the rise of cool mist on your face. Although Sandstone Falls is not a large cascade, the area is intriguing to children when they are shown the various rock formations and hollows carved out of the sandstone and conglomerate rock by centuries of rushing water.

A half mile from the campground or 14.5 miles from US-2, you reach the posted trailhead to Rainbow Falls. The 0.5-mile trail extends from the parking area to a long and somewhat steep stairway that ends at an observation platform above the cascade with a 40-foot drop. The falls are named for the mist that often reflects rainbows in the right angle of sunlight. The platform also provides an excellent view of the final leg of the Black River before it empties into Lake Superior.

APPENDIX:
QUICK TRAIL REFERENCE

Hike	Type	Length	Difficulty
Southeast Michigan			
1. Long Bark Trail	Interpretive walk	2 miles	Easy
2. Cherry Island Marsh Trail	Day hike	1.5 miles	Easy
3. North Bay Trail	Day hike	1.5 miles	Easy
4. Dolph Park Nature Area	Interpretive walk	0.5 mile	Easy
5. Wildwing Trail	Day hike	2.5 miles	Easy
6. Paint Creek Trail	Day hike	2.4 miles one-way	Moderate
7. Lakeshore and Springlake Trails	Day hike	2.4 to 3 miles	Moderate to challenging
8. Graham Lakes	Day hike	3.6 miles	Moderate
Heartland			
9. Bog Trail	Day hike	1.5 miles	Easy
10. Eastgate Connection	Day hike	2.7 miles	Moderate
11. Planet Walk	Interpretive walk	1 to 4 miles	Easy to moderate
12. Deer Run and Tallman Trails	Day hike	2 miles	Easy
13. The Ledges	Day hike	2 miles	Easy
14. Quarry Boardwalk	Day hike	1 mile	Easy
15. West Lake Wetland Walk and Bog Walk	Interpretive walk	1 to 3.5 miles	Easy to moderate
16. Graves Hill	Day hike	2 to 3 miles	Easy to moderate
17. Wetland Trail	Day hike	2 miles	Easy
18. Loda Lake Wildflower Sanctuary	Interpretive walk	1.5 miles	Easy
19. Pine Forest Pathway	Day hike	1 mile	Easy
20. Bowman Lake Trail	Day hike or overnight	2.5 miles	Easy
Lake Huron			
21. Sanilac Petroglyphs	Interpretive walk	1.5 miles	Easy
22. Huron Sand Dunes	Day hike	2.3 miles	Moderate
23. Shiawassee Waterfowl Trail	Day hike	5 miles	Moderate
24. Witch Hazel Trail and Lumberjack Loop	Interpretive walk	3 miles	Easy to moderate
25. Red Pine Pathway	Interpretive walk	1.5 miles	Easy
26. Highbanks Trail	Day hike	4 miles one-way	Moderate to challenging

terpretive enter?	Camping?	Fishing?	Swimming?	Highlights
es	No	No	No	Huron River
es	No	Yes	No	Birding
No	No	Yes	No	Island-hopping
No	No	No	No	Wildlife sightings
es	No	Yes	Yes	Blue heron rookery
es	No	Yes	No	Cider mill
es	No	Yes	Yes	Good shore fishing
No	No	Yes	No	Lake-studded area
es	No	No	No	Interesting bog
es	No	No	No	Red Cedar River
No	No	No	No	Walking from planet to planet
No	No	No	No	Brick Factory ruins
es	No	No	No	Rock climbers and cliffs
No	No	Yes	No	Good shore fishing
No	No	No	No	Walking through a bog
No	Yes	No	No	Climbing a "mountain"
No	No	No	No	Interesting swamp
No	No	No	No	Wildflowers
No	Yes	Yes	No	Old-growth white pine
No	Yes	Yes	No	Lakeshore camping
No	No	No	No	Ancient stone carvings
No	Yes	No	Yes	Sand dunes
No	No	No	No	Excellent birding
No	No	No	No	Giant pines
No	No	No	No	Old-growth red pines
es	Yes	No	No	Iargo Springs and AuSable River

Hike	Type	Length	Difficulty
Lake Huron (continued)			
27. Reid Lake	Day hike or overnight	4.2 miles	Moderate
28. Sinkholes Pathway	Day hike	2.4 miles	Easy to moder
29. Ocqueoc Falls Pathway	Day hike	3 miles	Moderate
30. Bell Townsite	Day hike	1 mile	Easy
31. North Bay Trail	Day hike	1.3 miles	Easy
32. Beaver Pond Trail	Interpretive walk	2 miles	Moderate
Lake Michigan			
33. Nipissing Dune Trails	Interpretive walk	3 miles	Moderate to challenging
34. Mud Lake Bog	Day hike	1 mile	Easy
35. Creek and Trillium Trails	Day hike	2.8 miles	Moderate
36. Big Tree and West Loops	Day hike	3.2 miles	Moderate
37. Mount Baldhead	Day hike	1 to 1.8 miles	Moderate
38. Dune Ridge Trail	Day hike	1 mile	Easy
39. Dune Climb Stairway	Day hike	1 mile	Easy
40. Silver Lake Sand Dunes	Day hike	3.6 miles	Moderate to challenging
41. Skyline Trail	Interpretive walk	1 mile	Easy
42. Nordhouse Dunes	Day hike	2.4 miles	Moderate
Northwest Michigan			
43. Platte Plains Trail	Overnight	3 to 7 miles	Easy to challenging
44. Empire Bluff Trail	Interpretive walk	2 miles	Moderate
45. Cottonwood Trail	Interpretive walk	1.5 miles	Easy
46. Dunes Trail	Day hike	4 miles	Easy to challenging
47. Sleeping Bear Point	Day hike	4 miles	Moderate
48. South Manitou Island	Day hike or overnight	6 miles	Easy to modera
49. Sand Lakes Quiet Area	Day hike or overnight	2.5 to 7.2 miles	Easy to modera
50. Skegemog Swamp Pathway	Day hike	2 miles	Easy
51. Sedge Meadow Trail	Interpretive walk	0.7 mile	Easy
52. Deadmans Hill	Day hike	3 miles	Moderate
53. AuSable River Trail	Interpretive walk	3 miles	Moderate
54. Avalanche Peak	Day hike	0.5 mile	Challenging
55. Balsam and Cedar Trails	Interpretive walk	1 mile	Easy
56. Mount Nebo and Big Stone Creek Trails	Day hike	3.9 to 4.6 miles	Moderate

terpretive nter?	Camping?	Fishing?	Swimming?	Highlights
o	Yes	Yes	No	Lakeshore camping
o	Yes	No	Yes	Limestone karsts
o	Yes	No	No	Waterfalls
o	No	No	Yes	Shipwreck and ghost town
o	No	No	No	Lighthouse
s	No	No	No	Water-powered sawmill
s	No	No	No	Cook Energy Information Center
o	No	No	No	Boardwalks across a bog
s	No	No	No	Old-growth beech-maple forest
o	No	Yes	No	Trout stream
o	No	No	Yes	Hand-powered ferry
o	No	No	Yes	View of Lake Michigan
s	Yes	No	Yes	Sand dunes
o	Yes	No	Yes	Hiking across sand dunes
s	Yes	Yes	Yes	View of Lake Michigan
o	Yes	No	Yes	Beautiful beaches
o	Yes	No	Yes	Beautiful beaches
o	No	No	No	Views of Lake Michigan
o	No	No	No	Pierce Stocking Scenic Drive
o	No	No	Yes	The Dune Climb
s	Yes	No	Yes	Searching for shipwrecks
s	Yes	No	Yes	Shipwrecks and a lighthouse
o	Yes	Yes	No	Lake-studded area
o	No	No	No	Birding
s	No	No	No	Marshes and cedar swamps
o	No	No	No	Jordon River Valley
s	Yes	Yes	No	Old-growth hemlock
o	No	No	No	Mountaintop views
s	No	No	Yes	Lake Michigan
o	Yes	Yes	Yes	Beaver ponds

Hike	Type	Length	Difficulty
Eastern Upper Peninsula			
57. Horseshoe Bay Wilderness	Day hike or overnight	2.5 miles	Moderate
58. Cut River Nature Trail	Day hike	1.5 to 2 miles	Moderate
59. Big Knob and Crow Lake Trails	Day hike	0.5 to 2.5 miles	Easy to mode
60. Pine Ridge Nature Trail	Interpretive walk	1.5 miles	Easy
61. Lower Tahquamenon Falls	Day hike	1 mile	Easy
62. AuSable Light Station	Day hike	3 miles	Easy
63. Miners Falls Trail	Interpretive walk	1.2 miles	Moderate
64. Tyoga Historic Pathway	Interpretive walk	1.4 miles	Easy
65. Ironjaw Semi-Primitive Area	Overnight	2 miles	Easy
66. Overlook Trail	Day hike	1.5 miles	Easy
67. Ninga Aki Pathway	Day hike	1.5 to 2.2 miles	Easy
68. Peninsula Point Nature Trail	Interpretive walk	2.5 to 3 miles	Easy
Western Upper Peninsula			
69. Sugarloaf Recreation Trail	Day hike	1.2 miles	Easy
70. Piers Gorge Trail	Day hike	3 miles	Moderate
71. Canyon Gorge Trail	Day hike	1 to 2 miles	Easy
72. Little Mountain Trail	Day hike	2.5 miles	Moderate
73. Tip Trail	Day hike	1.3 miles	Easy
74. Sturgeon Falls Trail	Day hike or overnight	1.5 miles	Moderate to challenging
75. Norway Lake Trail	Interpretive walk or overnight	1.2 miles	Easy
76. Beaver Lodge Trail	Interpretive walk	1.25 miles	Easy to mode
77. Cascade Falls Trail	Day hike	1.8 miles	Moderate
78. Government Peak Trail	Overnight	5.2 miles	Challenging
79. East and West River Trails	Day hike	2 miles	Moderate
80. Black River Falls	Day hike	0.2 to 0.8 mile one-way	Easy to mode

terpretive nter?	Camping?	Fishing?	Swimming?	Highlights
o	Yes	No	Yes	Beautiful beach
o	No	No	Yes	Cut River Gorge
o	Yes	No	Yes	Picking blueberries
s	No	No	No	Sighting wildlife
o	Yes	No	No	Waterfalls
s	Yes	No	No	Shipwrecks and a lighthouse
o	No	No	No	Waterfalls
o	No	No	No	History of lumberjacks
o	Yes	Yes	No	Backcountry shelter
s	Yes	No	Yes	Ghost town
o	Yes	No	Yes	Remote beach
o	No	No	No	Lighthouse
o	No	No	No	Mountaintop views
o	No	No	No	White water and rafters
o	No	No	No	Waterfalls
o	No	No	No	Mountaintop views
o	No	No	No	Views of Lake Superior
o	Yes	No	No	Sturgeon River Gorge
o	Yes	Yes	Yes	Walk-in campsites
o	Yes	Yes	Yes	Beaver ponds
o	No	No	No	Waterfalls
es	Yes	No	No	Backcountry shelter
o	Yes	No	No	Waterfalls
o	Yes	No	No	Waterfalls

INDEX

ABOUT THE AUTHOR AND PHOTOGRAPHER

Jim DuFresne is the author of *Michigan State Parks, Glacier Bay National Park*, and *Isle Royale National Park*. He writes a popular syndicated column called *Kidventures*, which covers Michigan's outdoor activities for families.

THE MOUNTAINEERS, founded in 1906, is a nonprofit outdoor activity and conservation club, whose mission is "to explore, study, preserve, and enjoy the natural beauty of the outdoors. . . ." Based in Seattle, Washington, the club is now the third-largest such organization in the United States, with 15,000 members and five branches throughout Washington State.

The Mountaineers sponsors both classes and year-round outdoor activities in the Pacific Northwest, which include hiking, mountain climbing, ski-touring, snowshoeing, bicycling, camping, kayaking and canoeing, nature study, sailing, and adventure travel. The club's conservation division supports environmental causes through educational activities, sponsoring legislation, and presenting informational programs. All club activities are led by skilled, experienced volunteers, who are dedicated to promoting safe and responsible enjoyment and preservation of the outdoors.

If you would like to participate in these organized outdoor activities or the club's programs, consider a membership in The Mountaineers. For information and an application, write or call The Mountaineers, Club Headquarters, 300 Third Avenue West, Seattle, Washington 98119; 206-284-6310.

The Mountaineers Books, an active, nonprofit publishing program of the club, produces guidebooks, instructional texts, historical works, natural history guides, and works on environmental conservation. All books produced by The Mountaineers fulfill the club's mission.

Send or call for our catalog of more than 500 outdoor titles:

The Mountaineers Books
1001 SW Klickitat Way, Suite 201
Seattle, WA 98134
800-553-4453
mbooks@mountaineers.org
www.mountaineersbooks.org

The Mountaineers Books is proud to be a corporate sponsor of Leave No Trace, whose mission is to promote and inspire responsible outdoor recreation through education, research, and partnerships. The Leave No Trace program is focused specifically on human-powered (non-motorized) recreation.

Leave No Trace strives to educate visitors about the nature of their recreational impacts, as well as offer techniques to prevent and minimize such impacts. Leave No Trace is best understood as an educational and ethical program, not as a set of rules and regulations.

For more information, visit *www.lnt.org*, or call 800-332-4100.